The Greatest Fox of Them All

The unauthorized inside revelations of a
Movie Magnate who defied The Establishment

THE
GREATEST FOX
OF THEM ALL

by Glendon Allvine

LYLE STUART, Inc. • New York

For Louise and Carole

The original Sunset & Western studios now used for television film productions.

TABLE OF CONTENTS

1

WHEN A MAN IS FIFTY

"WHEN a man reaches fifty," the film magnate was saying, "three courses lie ahead. He may dream of his past accomplishments, he may rest on his oars, or he may make ambitious plans for the future. The latter of these possibilities appeals to William Fox," said William Fox, who, like Napoleon, occasionally spoke of himself in the third person.

From the boat landing of Fox Hall, his estate at Woodmere, on Long Island, Nassau County, New York, the president of Fox Film Corporation, of which he personally owned 53 per cent, and of Fox Theatres, of which he owned 93 per cent, was speaking informally and confidently on October 12, 1929, to about thirty reporters invited to meet him for the first time since the motor car accident July 17, 1929, when his chauffeur was killed and William Fox almost died.

On that bright Columbus Day in 1929, God was in His Heaven, Herbert Hoover was in the White House, J. P. Morgan, George F. Baker and Albert H. Wiggin were in

Wall Street, and only film business, and not the atom, was split.

During three months in the hospital, and while recuperating at home, Fox had not been to his office in the Roxy Theatre. Nevertheless, his world-wide enterprises were flourishing, his new sound-on-film pictures were far ahead of competing films, and weekly business at the Roxy (demolished in 1960) was always more than $100,000.

In 1929 Fox owned more than a thousand theatres, and it galled him that Adolph Zukor topped him with about 1,200 in his Paramount companies.

There were only about a hundred Loew theatres, and Nicholas Schenck, president of Loew's and Metro-Goldwyn-Mayer, had arranged a secret peace conference at the Lakeville Country Club to try to stop Fox and Zukor in their suicidal race for power.

Fox liked fast driving, and his chauffeur was speeding the Rolls-Royce toward Great Neck just as a housewife, on a shopping trip in her Ford, reached an intersection simultaneously.

As his life hung in the balance, Fox had transfusions of blood of a rare type, supplied by a character actor who later was rewarded with a lifetime contract at the Fox studios.

In the crash the chauffeur was killed, but injuries to Jacob L. Rubenstein, riding with Fox, were less serious, and he was soon able to leave the hospital to return to his quarters over the Fox boathouse, where the big Fox yacht was anchored.

The meeting to arrange a theatre-buying truce between the two tycoons, thus violently interrupted, was never held.

Two years earlier, I had signed a five-year contract with

Fox as director of advertising and publicity. At that time Fox owned only two dozen theatres, and I was to get my gray hairs trying to keep up with the Fox world-wide expansion, and the transition from silent films to sound.

On October 11, 1929, a man from the Associated Press had telephoned me for confirmation of a rumor that William Fox had gone crazy, and I told him I'd check and see what I could find out. After the accident it was possible that brain trouble had developed, but I had not heard such a rumor. It might have been deliberately circulated by his enemies, for Fox was ruthless, and so were they.

When I got through to him at his house, he told me to call the AP back and deny the rumor.

"Yes, Mr. Fox, but isn't there a better way to handle this?"

"How would you do it?"

"I would see newspaper and trade paper people and let them judge for themselves."

"Do you think they'd be willing to come way out here?"

"Certainly," I said. "You are news."

"What'll I talk about?" he demanded.

"Tell them about your plans for the future," I suggested, and the next day I arrived at Fox Hall with six limousines full of eager newsmen from press associations, trade papers, financial publications and from what one of the divines at the Will Hays office used to call the lay press.

Fox began the press conference by referring to himself in the third person. "William Fox has invited you to his home today to tell you something of his plans for the next twenty-five years," said this former garment worker, born in Hungary January 1, 1879, and reared in such abject poverty that his family could not afford medical attention when the boy broke his left arm playing stickball on the streets of the lower East Side. His arm was crippled all his life.

As he warmed up he spoke so eloquently and so grammatically that nobody present would have known that he, like Shakespeare, had no formal schooling after the age of thirteen.

He spoke of the Tri-Ergon patents which he had acquired for $60,000 in Germany, the same patents that the United States Supreme Court would later sustain, presenting him with the right to collect damages from every theatre in the Western Hemisphere that had ever shown a sound-on-film picture, and making him, in effect, part owner of about fourteen thousand theatres in the United States which had been equipped for sound.

He noted with pride that a Movietone short just made in a Chicago hospital was the very first recording of surgery procedures for audio-visual teaching. He announced that he would produce 16-millimeter films for the teaching of science in high schools and colleges. He said he would make his variable-density, sound-on-film system available to churches, parish houses, temples and synagogues, so that the most eloquent religious leaders could be heard in houses of worship, large or small.

His Movietone newsreel crews, recording the march of events on six continents, were so far ahead of the four other newsreels that they never caught up with the Fox reel, and he announced that he was opening the world's first newsreel theatre, the Embassy, on Broadway next to the Palace, then in the dying days of vaudeville.

His Grandeur system was being developed on 80-millimeter films for wide screens, and *The Big Trail,* with

John Wayne, was already in production for showing on the huge Roxy screen. He was building five additional five-thousand-seat theatres in Brooklyn, Atlanta, Detroit, St. Louis, San Francisco.

As Fox paused for breath, a reporter asked: "How much will all this cost, Mr. Fox?"

"I have no idea," he answered candidly, "but I am prepared to give one fourth of my personal fortune to make it all come true."

"How much is this guy worth?" I heard the man from the *Sun* ask the man from the *Times,* who had done his homework and answered with more assurance than I could have ventured: "Thirty-six million dollars."

Current history was duly recorded the next morning on the first page of the *New York Times,* then, as now, a daily encyclopedia:

FOX AIMS TO REFORM
EDUCATION BY MOVIES

Producer To Spend $9,000,000
Over 25 Years To Substitute
Visual-Oral Schooling

Similar Aid For Church

Plans Talkies of Surgeons
To Aid Medical Study—
Film Libraries For Home Use

Later that October something happened to the stock market which economists are still explaining, and the nine million dollars that William Fox did not have a chance to apply to audio-visual education plummeted into a deficit of about a hundred million dollars owed to banks and investment houses and to the American Telephone and Telegraph Company through its subsidiary, Electrical Research Products, Inc.

His struggles to retain control of his theatrical empire, built from his $1,600 savings invested in a Brooklyn nickelodeon, have been detailed in *Upton Sinclair Presents William Fox,* a passionate book denouncing Wall Street bankers and lawyers. It makes fascinating reading today with Ferdinand Lundberg's demonstration in his *The Rich and the Super-Rich* that the concentration of wealth in the Rockefeller and other financial dynasties is greater than it was a third of a century ago.

With the biographee long in his grave, the peppery Sinclair, after publishing ninety books, one for each of his years, carried on his crusades for social justice until he died November 25, 1968. Few of his works have had more gusto than the book he wrote, published and promoted in 1933 with such movie-type copy as this:

> A Melodrama of Fortune, Conflict and Triumph. Packed with Thrills and Heart Throbs. East Side Boy Conquers Fame and Power. The Masters of Millions Envy His Triumph and Plot His Downfall. The Octopus Battles the Fox. The Duel of a Century: The Sensation of a Lifetime!
>
> Never in Screen History has there been a Feature so Stupendous as This. An Inside Story, a First-Hand Revelation of Politics and Finance, with a Ten Billion Dollar Cast of Statesmen and Financiers.
>
> At the same time a Story for the Family, tense and moving with Love, Loyalty and a Woman's Soul. A Romance so Fine, so True, so loaded with Laughter and Tears, that none can resist it.

Charles Evans Hughes, later appointed chief justice of the United States Supreme Court, was one of the battery of lawyers engaged by Fox to fight his battles. Most of my dealings were with the aging Samuel Untermyer who, from his bed in his suite at the Hotel Ambassador on Park Avenue (now an office building), used to breathe defiance at the telephone company.

During the stockholder fights in the spring of 1930, when nobody knew who owned control of Fox Films and Fox Theatres, I issued daily statements impartially for the principal contenders, Bancamerica-Blair and Lehman Brothers in the mornings, Halsey Stuart in the afternoons and William Fox, through Untermyer, in the evenings. Leaving Sarah Siegel and my female secretariat to the day shift, I worked nights with Elliot McManus, who took notes and typed out mimeographed releases as we gave the telephone company hell.

Why?

Because John E. Otterson, president of Electrical Research Products, Inc., which manufactured and serviced talking picture equipment under disputed patents, was, with bulldog tenacity, determined to get Fox out and take over his companies for AT&T and its subsidiary Western Electric.

Because Otterson and ERPI refused to recognize the Tri-Ergon patents controlled by William Fox, or to pay license fees for the use of the unique fly-wheel sprocket device, while insisting on collecting stiff royalties for their own patent pool.

Because Untermyer knew that everybody (stockholders excepted) who got a wrong number or lost a coin in a slot or was overcharged on a bill, disliked the telephone company, and he was determined to get the AT&T out of the film business, since it was sufficiently monopolistic in communications. It took years, and Untermyer died before he could chew the victory cake, but his persistent agitation finally made the octopus disgorge its ERPI along with all its equipment and activities in the field of sound films, as well as its Long Island City studios, acquired after Paramount went into bankruptcy to satisfy the AT&T's claims against that company.

As the battle ranged back and forth, I remember one day in December, 1929, when Otterson seemed to have won out, having become head man in a trusteeship trio, along with Harry Leonard Stuart, to whose investment house twelve million dollars were owed, when it was obvious that these two could always outvote the third trustee, William Fox.

Coming for the first time over to the Hell's Kitchen head office at 850 Tenth Avenue, "that flag lieutenant," as Fox called the 1904 graduate of the United States Naval Academy, asked for the keys to the vault and the consolidated balance sheets, but nobody could find them or had the authority to surrender the records.

That was the day nobody knew nuttin at Fox Fillum. (When I first joined the company I explained to the veteran head telephone operator that it was a one-syllable word, but she persisted in the habit of a lifetime and, while I was willing to battle the telephone company, I elected not to fight the solidly entrenched operator.)

When Otterson came back the next day and found the vault still locked and the general counsel, Saul E. Rogers, unavailable, he retired, on advice of his own lawyers, and neither he nor Stuart was ever able to function as trustee.

William Fox, meanwhile, had holed in at his Woodmere estate, too sick to talk to anybody, and for six weeks he

was incommunicado. Not even his distinguished personal
attorney, Charles Evans Hughes, could penetrate the
renardine curtain.

Never before had Charles Evans Hughes represented
such an unpredictable and cantankerous individual. When
he had negotiated a trusteeship agreement which averted
bankruptcy, he had naturally assumed that such details
as financial records, corporate signatures and keys to the
vaults would be forthcoming. This was the nadir for the
bearded Baptist who soon afterward reached his peak—
as chief justice of the United States Supreme Court.

Not until four months later, with the simultaneous
passing of keys and records to representatives of the Chase
National Bank and the first of five annual payments of
half a million dollars to William Fox, was the management turned over to Harley Lyman Clarke, who had made
a fortune in utility promotions with Samuel Insull, and
who was president of Utilities Power and Light Company.

By this maneuvering William Fox got from the bankers
an additional amount of $2,500,000 for his services
for the next five years as chairman of the Advisory Committee, a purely legal device.

Harry Reichenbach, industry wit and kibitzer, noted:
"By the time this committee has its first meeting, all you
gentlemen will have long white beards."

Clarke brought with him from Chicago his own director
of public relations, who succeeded me when my employment contract, with six months to go, was paid in full.
The new man installed as his assistant a young woman
new to show business.

In 1928 there was a charming little tearoom in the
Fifties just off Fifth Avenue, operated by two charming
young ladies who served luncheon and afternoon tea to a

discriminating clientele. Since the rent was high and no liquor was served illegally, the capacity small and the service leisurely, an economist might have wondered how these young ladies made out financially, and there were indeed some distinguished economists who did their mid-day refueling at this address.

Whenever Harley Clarke was in New York from Chicago, "that reader of gas meters" used to lunch there with the New England Brahmin, Albert H. Wiggin, head of the Chase National Bank and of its corporate twin, the Chase Securities Company, and confer with these girls.

In the caverns of Wall Street, lawyers and fiscal agents handled details, but it was here in the relaxed atmosphere of Harley's Hideaway that the head of America's then greatest bank and the Insull satellite involved themselves and their companies in the Fox and Clarke enterprises for a total of almost a hundred million dollars.

Here Clarke and Wiggin manipulated the stock of General Theatres Equipment, Inc. (a holding company incorporated July 11, 1929, in Delaware, with general offices at 624 South Michigan Avenue, Chicago), until its stock reached a 1929 high of $66. Its 1,800,000 shares were controlled by three certificates which had a total face value of nine dollars. Clarke owned one of these shares, Samuel Insull another and Harry L. Stuart the third. Three similar shares, one each owned by the same promoters, also controlled Utilities Power and Light Company of Chicago, worth at that time more than half a billion dollars.

After the stock market crash, when the Clarke and Fox enterprises were so deflated and entangled that banks and brokers and investment houses were in peril, the manipulation of General Theatres Equipment stocks and bonds by Chase Securities Corporation and its associated underwriters drove into bankruptcy the Philadelphia banking house of West & Company, established one year after the signing of the Declaration of Independence, and the old Boston firm of W. S. Hammons & Company and Pynchon & Company of New York, whose twenty-eight partners were ruined.

Now all hell broke loose and the Rockefellers in 1930 got rid of the Boston Brahmin whom they had trusted to run the Chase companies.

With Rockefeller money, the Chase Bank wrote off the Wiggin errors and replaced him as president with John D. Rockefeller's brother-in-law, Winthrop W. Aldrich. In 1929 the Chase Securities Company had traded in stocks with $450,000,000 of bank deposits, and Owen D. Young agreed with Samuel Untermyer that such use of bank moneys was reckless and dangerous. Ever since 1913, as counsel to the Pujo Committee investigation of the money trust, when Untermyer interrogated George F. Baker about the stock manipulations of his First National Bank, the crusading lawyer had been hammering away at these bank affiliates, which were finally outlawed during the first term of Franklin D. Roosevelt.

Christmas in 1929 was hardly a day of cheer for millions of Americans who had lost their stake and faith in capitalism after the stock market crash in October, for now many of them were losing their homes through mortgage foreclosure. With banks failing and corporations by the thousands, big and little, falling into bankruptcy, President Herbert Hoover and his Administration were desperately trying to avert national disaster.

William Fox, whose ideology always adjusted to financial self-interest, was an ardent Tammany Democrat along with his general manager, Winfield Sheehan in New York City, but nationally, with Hoover in the White House, he was a Republican.

On Christmas day, 1929, the chairman of the Republican National Committee dined at the home of the chairman of the Board of the biggest bank in America (and in the world) with assets of more than two billion dollars. And what were these gentlemen discussing on that holy day? William Fox, what else?

Colonel Claudius F. Huston was saying that in the public interest and to avert colossal bankruptcy of the Fox companies, the president of the United States would consider it a personal favor if the Chase National Bank would extend further credit to these prosperous companies, until long-range financing could be arranged. He reported to Wiggin that he had failed in his attempt to interest Henry Ford (the original) in helping Fox, thinking he might enlist sympathetic interest for another up-from-the-work-bench pioneer whose empire looked good to the banks. After thinking it over, the canny Ford decided to stick to his Model A.

Now Huston, as a presidential envoy, was laying it on the line: If Wiggin of Chase would pass the magic word along to other bankers and let Fox have temporary financing, the president of the United States would personally appreciate this help. His host, next to J. P. Morgan the biggest money man in the U.S., slept on it overnight and the next day sent to the president this terse message:

"I resent your interference on behalf of Fox; mind your own business."

In sworn testimony to the Senate November 28, 1933, Wiggin called this report "absolutely and entirely false." His testimony also revealed that he had lost $1,572,752 in trading in Harley Clarke's General Theatres Equipment, Inc.

The 1930 financial troubles of the prosperous Fox companies grew out of a combination of technological change from the pantomimic silents, which were immensely profitable with vernacular titles added anywhere in the world; plus theatre acquisitions pyramided just before a national depression, when bankers, who also had been gambling on an expanding economy, suddenly began calling their loans.

This financial squeeze came just fifteen years after William Fox had gone public with the incorporation of Fox Film Corporation, February 1, 1915. Without supplying any new cash, but contributing his compulsive drive and canny insight into the public acceptance of feature pictures with the decline of vaudeville, he threw in his leases and ownership of ten theatres in Brooklyn, Manhattan and The Bronx plus a dozen in the hinterlands, his real estate on both sides of Western Avenue on Sunset Boulevard in Hollywood, his vaudeville booking company and Box Office Attractions, his national distributing offices.

With insurance and banking money provided by the McCarter, Kuser and Usar families of Newark and the small New Jersey investment house of Eisele and King, Fox Film Corporation was launched on the New York Stock Exchange, becoming the first film company so listed. This common stock was a bonus, issued fifty-fifty to William Fox and his New Jersey bankers, and shared equally in dividend payments with the 500,000 preferred voting shares originally owned equally by Fox and the banking group.

As treasurer of the new company, John Eisele nursed finances along so soundly that, two years later, one of the investors decided to cash in on his substantial profits. A delighted William Fox was able to buy this 3 per cent of voting stock, which gave him voting control.

Such was the driving energy of Fox and his general manager Winnie Sheehan and the two brothers of Mrs. Fox, Jack and Joe Leo, that the new company was soon able to retire the preferred stock held by the Jersey group, and these men grew enormously wealthy from dividends and from trading as the stock peaked in 1928 at $119.62½.

It was this 53 per cent voting control, plus the William Fox 93 per cent control of Fox Theatres (incorporated November 5, 1925), that was at issue in the 1930 battle of Wall Street, when Clarence M. Dillon, of Dillon, Read & Co., conspired with Wiggin of the Chase Bank to capture the Fox companies.

While Fox was in control of the companies, he served without salary as president. He also had personal holdings in various related corporations such as:

1. The real estate brokerage company, Foxthal, whose 10 per cent commissions were equally split with A. C. Blumenthal and Fox Theatres.

2. Grandeur, Inc., the wide-screen process equally owned by Harley Clarke and William Fox.

3. American Tri-Ergon Corporation, 90 per cent owned by William Fox, who had personally gambled $60,000 to acquire Western Hemisphere rights to these Swiss-German patents controlled for the rest of the world by the Swiss Tri-Ergon Company.

The fly-wheel patent 1713726 and the double print patent were being used in more than 14,000 theatres equipped not only by the telephone company's ERPI but with the variable area sound-on-film system manufactured by the Radio Corporation of America, and actively promoted competitively by David Sarnoff, who scorned the uncouth William Fox.

Every sound picture produced in the United States had violated these patents, according to Ward, Crosby and Neal, attorneys for Tri-Ergon, who on March 19, 1931, filed a complaint in the Federal Court, Delaware District, asking the court to declare patent infringements by Electrical Research Products, Inc., Altoona Publix Theatres, Wilmer and Vincent and other exhibitors.

After studying the highly technical devices and laboratory procedures and listening to arguments presented by attorneys for ERPI on the double print patents and RCA on the flywheel patent, the court decided that these patents were not valid for want of invention.

An appeal was taken and on November 28, 1933, Judge Albert W. Johnson, sitting in the United States District Court in Scranton, Pennsylvania, ruled that the patents were valid and established the right of American Tri-Ergon to collect damages from every producer and theatre owner in the United States, Canada and Latin America.

This ruling was, of course, appealed, and on June 13, 1934, the United States Circuit Court upheld the District Court, confirming that both patents were valid, and that the Radio Corporation of America and the American Telephone and Telegraph Company, through Western Electric and ERPI, had for six years been violating the Fox patents.

These two corporate giants took an appeal to the United States Supreme Court and what seemed to be a final judicial determination came October 8, 1934, when the associate justices of the highest court (Chief Justice Charles Evans Hughes abstaining) decided unanimously that the Circuit Court was right, and ordered it to in-

struct United States District Courts to name special
masters or referees to decide on damages for these millions of dollars of patent infringements.

When this sensational good news was telephoned by
General Counsel Saul E. Rogers to William Fox at his
office in the Roxy Theatre, a friend happened to be in
the office and later reported to me that William Fox exclaimed in his supreme moment of triumph:

"Now I've got the sonsabitches by the balls, and don't
think I won't twist them."

Years later, when I checked with Rogers on this telephone call, he reported the identical phrase, which is not
easily forgotten.

The on-the-scene reporter gave further fascinating details, relating that the man who now practically owned
the entire American moving picture industry got up
from his desk and danced a jig on Roxy's ornate rug.

At the height of Adolph Hitler's greatest victory, after
the fall of Czechoslovakia, the world saw with its own
eyes that Hitler danced a jig, because the most memorable
of newsreel moments was shown throughout the world
on Fox Movietone News. It was not until 1956 that one
of the newsreel boys confessed his fake: Der Führer had
just been rambling along in some rather dull library
footage when a clever film editor, working on his movie-
ola, snipped frames together until his film jigsaw became
a jigstep.

No camera recorded the Fox step, but his jig was up.
He should never have sent 14,000 warning letters to exhibitors, or published ads in the trade papers reminding
theatre owners that every projection of any sound picture
was a patent violation. This publication was used by at-

torneys for Paramount as documentary evidence that Fox was coercing producers and distributors.

In October, 1934, injunction and accounting actions against all producers, including Fox Film Corporation, were entered by Tri-Ergon in the states where the companies were incorporated. Paramount and RKO were in bankruptcy, and their attorneys appealed to the Supreme Court to reconsider the patent decision which placed an intolerable additional burden on these distressed companies. On November 6, 1934, the United States Supreme Court agreed to review the patent decision, but specified that no new evidence was to be allowed in Tri-Ergon arguments.

All of these appeals, not only from Wall Street lawyers, but pressures from United States senators and from representatives of theatre owners, seem to have jolted nine old men into an awareness of the meaning of their supreme judgment. Was it possible that these learned judges did not understand the significance of what they were deciding when they refused to issue that June, 1934, certiorari? Did not a single one of nine wise men realize that they were putting the entire motion picture industry into the clutches of one man? Were they so intent on legal niceties and narrow applications that the substance of the Circuit Court decision eluded them? Did somebody from Wall Street have to explain the meaning of their decision to a judge relaxing at a Washington cocktail party?

Just twenty-two weeks after these Supreme Court justices had voted unanimously that the Tri-Ergon patents were valid, these same solons met on March 14, 1935, and decided that, in the public interest, these same patents were not valid.

These were Harding and Coolidge and Hoover justices,

so violently denounced later by Franklin D. Roosevelt when they refused to die or resign so that he could shape the court to his liking.

When Fox paid $60,000 for 90 per cent of the Tri-Ergon Western Hemisphere patents he also acquired an option to buy remaining world rights for $40,000, and in his emergency he offered to sell these patents to the American Telephone and Telegraph Company for $25,000,000, but "that flag lieutenant" Otterson refused to pay more than $5,000,000.

Into this impasse stepped Saul E. Rogers, the general counsel who had broken with Fox in the 1930 upheaval, and softened up Otterson so that he offered $7,500,000. Fox, always a sharp trader, then demanded $30,000,000. Now that he was gambling for really high stakes, Fox consulted the eminent Philadelphia lawyer George Wharton Pepper, who decided that they had the telephone company on the ropes, and advised him to hold out for $50,000,000.

After the United States Supreme Court decision in March, 1935, this fifty million dollars added up to zero, and Fox was personally out of pocket more than two million dollars in legal fees, and had claims against him, in the sallow and worried flesh, totaling seventeen million dollars.

Whose scrotum now, as the octopus spreads its tentacles and squeezes?

2

MAGNASCOPE

Jesse Lasky glows to other people's ideas; knows how to expand them, make them practicable.

—WILL IRWIN

THE first time I saw William Fox was in the lobby of the Rivoli Theatre on Broadway at four o'clock on the afternoon of December 7, 1926. I was handling public relations for Paramount at the time. Fox had dropped everything to arrive at that Paramount theatre with Winfield R. Sheehan, his vice president and general manager, to see what the opposition was up to, because the *New York Times* and other newspapers were all commenting on the Magnascope, the first expanding wide screen, which had caused such excitement the night before.

While I had high hopes for the effect that I had devised and rehearsed and titled to hop up an ailing silent feature titled *Old Ironsides,* I had no idea that my dramatic application of this wide-angled lens would project such industry turmoil, start a trend toward wide screens and impel William Fox to begin building 5,000-seat theatres.

Jesse L. Lasky had asked me to listen to audience reaction during the intermission of that second performance

of *Old Ironsides,* and when I heard what Fox had to say
I realized that my little gimmick was a pebble tossed
into a placid lake, causing ripples and circles and rever-
berations from Broadway to Hollywood.

It all began one day in October when Lasky, vice
president of the Famous Players-Lasky Corporation, summoned me to his office in the Paramount Building. I had
been detached from the publicity department, had my
salary doubled, and was then, in my eighth year with
Paramount, sort of a public relations trouble shooter.

Now Lasky confided to me that he was in trouble with
Old Ironsides, which had been budgeted at a million
dollars and completed, by a director earning a thousand
dollars a day, at a cost of $2,200,000.

"There's a million dollars worth of fog in this picture,"
he said, referring to the bad weather that had kept a large
cast and crew idle as a replica of the 44-gun frigate
U.S. Constitution tossed sunless in Pacific waters for
more than a month.

"See if you can't figure out a way to sell this picture
so that we can get our money back."

During two weeks in October I ran this silent picture
every day and tried to devise some promotional way out.
Then I remembered that there was a wide-angled lens in
the Bausch and Lomb catalog, which had been brought
to my attention that spring by Laurence Del Riccio
when he was passed along to me from Lasky's office.
Del Riccio was looking for a job, and during our ten-
minute talk he mentioned this lens, which he said could
be used to project big pictures on outdoor screens. If
either of us had been in the groove that spring of 1926
and had settled down to some intensive brain-storming,
we might have devised the drive-in theatre, but it was

two decades before Richard M. Hollingshead, Jr., thought of that idea and started a new industry, so that in 1968 there were more than 4,400 motorized cinemas in operation, accounting for one-fourth of the total film rentals in the United States.

Now, some six months later, I thought that, if we could launch the vessel on the regular screen and keep it coming toward the audience on an expanded screen, we might get an exciting effect. When I explained my idea to Lasky and asked him to have all the film cutouts from the launching scene shipped to New York from the Hollywood studio, I said that while we were waiting for the film I would order a screen built as wide as the Rivoli proscenium arch, doubling to forty feet the width of the existing screen.

"Can you do that?"

"I don't know of any law against it."

"But if it's practical, why hasn't it been done before?"

"Because of the balcony overhang. The screen is as high as vision from the last row in the orchestra will permit, and the width is proportionate."

"Have you any idea how much all this will cost?"

"Around two thousand dollars."

After all these years I still remember his laugh as he said:

"After two million two, what's two thousand dollars? Go ahead and see what you can do. I'll wire Hollywood for the cutouts."

Three decades later, in the same proscenium arch in the same theatre, at a cost of more than a quarter of a million dollars, Michael Todd installed a curved screen of the same width for the world premiere of *Oklahoma!*

While my huge screen was being built, I engaged

Hugo Riesenfeld, for a fee of $5,000, to compose and assemble and orchestrate a score, with the insistence that he build to a crescendo, wide open on all the brass and strings and percussions, as the screen expanded.

When the cutouts arrived, I stretched out the launching scene as far as it would go, and took the sequence out of the second reel and fitted it into the end of the sixth for the regular lens, and onto the beginning of the seventh reel for the wide-angled lens. When the vessel slid right into the laps of the audience, the title read: "Intermission: Ten Minutes."

Two nights before the opening date I invited the big four at Paramount, Adolph Zukor, Jesse Lasky, Sidney Kent and Walter Wanger, to come to a midnight demonstration. Starting the picture just before the intermission reel, I pressed the signal to backstage, and the well-rehearsed stagehands parted the curtains slowly as Old Ironsides slid right into the skeptical quartet. They were amazed.

"Do it again," said Adolph Zukor, and as we rewound they scattered to various parts of the theatre, Zukor sitting by himself in the last row. We projected the sequence again and it came out on cue.

"No good," Zukor announced.

"Why not?" Lasky wanted to know.

"You can't see the picture from the last three rows. That's $300 we lose at every full house."

"Except for some holiday Saturday nights I can't remember when we ever had a capacity house at the Rivoli," Lasky replied.

Wanger suggested that we go next door to Lindy's and talk things out over a cup of coffee. Not until four in the morning did Zukor agree to try it out on an audience. I asked them to keep the whole project a secret, so that nobody except the house crew would know we were testing an innovation. I wanted the Magnascope to take them by surprise. The first half of the picture, with Esther Ralston and George Bancroft, was on the placid side. Just before intermission I held my breath as I pushed the signal button to part the curtains on the switchover. It worked! Two thousand people stood up and cheered. A yellowed clipping from the *New York Times* reports:

"The scene that ended the first half of the picture was a startling surprise, for the standard screen disappeared and the whole stage, from proscenium arch to the boards, was filled with a moving picture of Old Ironsides. This brought every man and woman in the audience to their feet. Following the intermission, most of the scenes of Old Ironsides were depicted by this apparatus, a device discovered by Glen Allvine of the Famous Players-Lasky Corporation. Mr. Allvine said that he called the idea or invention a magnascope. It is a magnifying lens attached to the ordinary projection machine. This wide-angle lens was extremely effective."

Quinn Martin, film reviewer for the *New York World*, reported: "When 'Old Ironsides' lurched nearer and nearer to the orchestra pit, to burst with an orchestral roar into what appeared to be life size, seemingly over the very heads of the audience, some naval officers, including the Secretary of the Navy, abandoned their seats for the time being and gave a number of whoops. The scene really deserved the hand. I'll offer two to one Calvin Coolidge would have tossed off a cheer."

It was reviews such as this that had caused William Fox and Winfield Sheehan to get over to that first matinee. A capacity house at the second showing again stood up and cheered as the ship slid right into their laps. I was all ears in the lobby during intermission, and was thrilled with what I heard Fox tell Sheehan. I recognized them from their pictures in the trade papers, but they did not know me as I eavesdropped on them.

"I tell you, Winnie, this is going to revolutionize theatre business. Don't you see, we've got to give them big pictures, or people will stay at home and look at little pictures on radio beams. [On June 13, 1925, C. Francis Jenkins had demonstrated Vision-by-Radio, and no technical advance went unnoted by William Fox.] From now on, Winnie, I'm going to build all my theatres with big screens and 5,000 seats." (He did, in Brooklyn, Atlanta, Detroit, St. Louis, San Francisco.)

"Find out how this thing works. The *Times* this morning has the name of the man who cooked it up. Get him in to see me right away."

The next day I had a call from Sheehan, and I met him at the Savoy-Plaza, that charming hotel which General Motors has sabotaged. He said that the Fox companies were expanding tremendously, and how would I like to work for Fox? I was coy, since I had overheard Fox tell him to hire me, and I said that I liked Paramount, where I dealt directly with the president and vice president. Sheehan said that he would give me a contract, and that I would report directly to him and Fox, and that the possibilities for me were unlimited. We parted with the understanding that we would resume the discussion later.

When I got back to Paramount, Lasky sent for me.

"Well, the Magnascope certainly got results," I gloated.

"Yes, much bigger than anybody figured," he said. "So big I'm in a jam with the studio. Ben Schulberg is furious. He says we had no right to edit the picture."

"But you told me to go ahead and work with the studio cutouts."

"Yes, I know, but I had forgotten about a clause in Ben's contract that says nobody is to touch the completed picture after he has approved its final editing."

"But with the Magnascope you may get your money back on *Old Ironsides*."

"That may be, but all the reviews are about the Magnascope; it overwhelms the picture. Mr. Zukor agrees with Ben. He says we should never have put it on the big screen. You remember how we had to talk him into it that night at Lindy's. Now Zukor and Schulberg are lined up against me and Wanger."

"And Kent?"

"He's neutral."

"I'm sorry about these developments, but audiences are getting a big thrill out of the Magnascope at every performance."

"Zukor isn't, and Schulberg is out for blood. He says you've got to go. No hurry, but I think you'd better look around."

And so I doubled my salary by signing a five-year contract with Fox.

When Merian Cooper came back from Siam, after having stampeded a thousand elephants in front of Ernest Schoedsack's camera, he realized that all those elephants, charging into an expanding screen, would double the thrill of his fabulous *Chang*, which was the second picture to use the Magnascope, and with even more spectacular success.

Although Paramount lawyers had assured Lasky and me that the effect could not be patented, Paramount was granted eighteen patents on the Magnascope. All these patents have now expired, and other lenses and projectors have been engineered for big screens.

Magnascope antedated by thirty years Zukor's belated VistaVision, which was an attempt to avoid buying the Skouras CinemaScope lenses and screens.

Zukor had rejected this same wide screen squeeze lens when it was first demonstrated at the 1939 New York World's Fair by its inventor, Dr. Henri Cretien.

While they were in Europe in 1953 investigating Eidophor, another Swiss invention, Earl Sponable, the Fox inventor of Movietone, reminded Spyros Skouras at the London airport of this squeeze lens, and Skouras impetuously flew back to Switzerland to confront the amazed Dr. Cretien, who then came into a belated new career after a sudden deal was made for CinemaScope.

All of these techniques, of course, were catapulted into reality by attempts to simplify and improve the three-projector, two-streak Cinerama, which the Paramount special effects man, Fred Waller, had developed at Zukor's old Long Island City studios.

With optical refinements and new laboratory techniques for processing color film, we have advanced from the crude Magnascope through Cinerama to Ultra-Vision to Ultra Panavision 70 and Dimension 80 and other projection systems for all sizes of film. Further refinements in huge color pictures are now in the making in an attempt to pull people into theatres and away from Vision-by-Radio, that tiny moving picture, fragmented by commercials, that makes it so easy to relax at home.

3

UP FROM LINING COATS

The cinema is an invention without a future.

—LOUIS AND AUGUSTE LUMIERE, INVENTORS OF THE
CINEMATOGRAPHE

WILLIAM FOX was always a wary and suspicious individual, and not without reason when he discovered that he was being swindled by J. Stuart Blackton, president of the Vitagraph Company of America, who had appointed a handsome slicker to unload the Brooklyn nickelodeon at 200 Broadway that the mighty Vitagraph no longer needed. Even though Fox may never have heard of caveat emptor, he got the idea.

When he appeared twice by appointment to inspect the 146-chair storeroom, Fox found a steady stream of ticket buyers, for the agent was paying them to see the show. Gulled into buying this salted nickelodeon, he discovered, when his hard-earned savings of $1,600 had passed, that there were only two customers on the opening day, and that this very thin dime would not pay for his doorman, let alone film rental.

In this emergency he hired a magician, in high hat and satin breeches, to do tricks outside the theatre and then invite the crowd that collected to come on inside and see the show upstairs without charge.

It's a long, long way from Brooklyn's Broadway to Times Square Broadway, but in half a century the techniques of ballyhoo and the sidewalk pitch men have not changed.

In August, 1967, when a nervous Fox film was playing the Forum at the 47th Street corner of Broadway in Manhattan, the boys in the advertising department hired a stilt-walker to strut back and forth on the crowded sidewalk and hand out heralds urging pedestrians to spend $3.00 to see the picture. Ballyhoo was right back where it was half a century ago, but the price of movie admission had gone up 6,000 per cent.

When his first theatre was making a profit, after a week of free shows, Fox parlayed that profit into a second theatre, and the second into a third, and before long he had twenty-five of these common shows, which was legal phrasing for places with fewer than 299 seats and so not subject to fire regulations prevailing in larger theatres.

Although he made a point of meeting his notes and impressing bankers with his hard work and reliability, he played hunches with a clarity of vision that eluded his more erudite lawyers and bankers.

Shrewd, suspicious, trusting nobody except his family, he was fast and flexible as he clawed his way to the top. Twice—at the beginning of his career and at the end— he defied entrenched vested interests and fought legal battles that were sustained in the highest courts in the land. His stunning victory in 1912, after four years of litigation to enforce the Sherman Anti-Trust Act, knocked out the right of the Motion Pictures Patents Company to collect fees for the use of all cameras and projectors and put an end to licensed Kalem, Selig, Edison, Lubin, Biograph, Pathé, Essanay and even the great Vitagraph Company of America.

Into this vacuum, free to make and show pictures as they liked, moved Universal, Loew, Famous Players and Fox's own Box Office Attractions Film Rental Company, which developed into Fox Films and Fox Theatres.

At first Fox was content to distribute films that other people made and to concentrate on being an exhibitor. For an outlay of $20,000, he remodeled an old burlesque theatre at 194 Grand Street in Brooklyn into the Comedy Theatre for vaudeville and films and acquired The Folly in Brooklyn and The Star on Lexington Avenue and 107th Street in Manhattan.

It was at the City Theatre on East Fourteenth Street that he became a partner with the Tammany politicians "Big Tim" and "Little Tim" Sullivan, and from then on he never had any trouble with Fire Department regulations for his theatres. On the contrary, the secretary to the Fire Commissioner, Winfield R. Sheehan, saw a bigger future with Fox than with Tammany, and became his long-time associate.

Fox sold off his twenty-five store shows, remodeled existing vaudeville houses and built new moving picture theatres, until in 1920 he had a prosperous chain of twelve in the four most populous boroughs of New York and a dozen other theatres in the hinterland. A decade later these were expanded into the Fox Metropolitan circuit of about 175 houses.

Sheehan established distribution centers in London, Dublin, Paris, Berlin and Rome, and moved on to Australia and around the world to set up what is still the top distribution system in the picture business. Although he always kept his eye on overseas distribution, and scouted talent and stories annually in Europe, he left management to his younger brother Clayton, who traveled with his wife on expense accounts, lived simply, saved his money and was all set to nurse along his nonfilm stocks when the bankers liquidated the Foxes and the Sheehans.

With his Tammany and newspaper associations he opened up world-wide vistas for the somewhat parochial Fox, and lined up insurance money which flowed from Newark for expansion into Hollywood real estate and production.

As a newspaper man he found pleasure in establishing the Fox newsreel and turned its operation over to Truman Talley, a reporter he had known on the *New York Herald*. As vice president and general manager he kept an eye on production of silent pictures at the Sunset and Western studios in Hollywood, but day-to-day operations were in the hands of Sol Wurtzel, who, as former secretary to William Fox, could be trusted to keep costs down and to deal with the Altman relatives who supplied furniture and properties for the sets.

During the silent era a steady flow of unpretentious, sentimental and folksy pictures issued from the Fox studios, without the reaching for art and biography that occasionally varied the menu at Paramount and Warner Brothers. Tom Mix was the cowboy star, Theda Bara vamped in forty pictures in three years and *Over the Hill to the Poorhouse* was advertised as "the greatest human drama of all time."

And who shall say that Theda Bara's 1917 *Cleopatra*, the script of which President Spyros Skouras commended to Producer Walter Wanger, was not a better commercial venture for Fox than the Elizabeth Taylor fiasco? These *Cleopatra* troubles of Twentieth Century-Fox came after the death of the nineteenth century Fox.

On the first day of the new century, which also happened to be his twenty-first birthday, William Fox married the sixteen-year-old Eve Leo, and with all their ups and downs they always celebrated this triple holiday together. Their happiest days, they agreed, were in their $11-a-month honeymoon flat in Brooklyn.

In 1899 Fox was earning $17 a week as head of the lining department of S. Cohen & Son. He worked eleven hours a day six days a week, but only five hours on Sunday. To support a wife Fox told his employer that he would need higher wages, and was told that he was already overpaid. When he had made his millions and S. was just another Cohen, Fox used to enjoy telling this story and agreeing that Cohen was right.

"It would have been so easy to spend all that I saved in those days. Every penny was something that I denied myself, with the thought in mind that if I was going forward I had to have money. I saw that capital was what I needed. Either I had to be content to work for someone else all my life, or fight for independence. The latter course made it necessary to deny myself everything I could possibly contrive to do without until I had accomplished my aim and could afford to permit myself the things I missed.

"My father described his lack of progress by saying he never had an opportunity to save. He was married when he came to this country and could never earn more than it took to keep his family. My mother encouraged me to save, and I can recall many occasions when she thanked me for offering her an extra dollar or two that I had earned, but said she would much rather I put it in the bank. I still have the original account in the Drydock Savings Bank," he told Upton Sinclair three decades later. "That book is one of my proud possessions to this day."

With another workman earning $25 a week at the Cohen establishment, he went into partnership in the Knickerbocker Cloth Examining and Shrinking Company. With Fox out getting business and his partner examining cloth, they barely got through their first year, but in the second year they made a profit of $10,000. With this business record he was able to borrow enough money from the German Exchange Bank to buy out his partner, who, like later partners, could not adjust to the frantic Fox pace.

As the sole owner, Fox, the lone wolf, with the help of his wife, the lioness, examined and shrank cloth until, by relentless hard work, he had made a profit of $50,000, and was able to sell at a substantial profit his little company with the big name.

FADE OUT forever on shrinking cloth and lining coats, and

FADE IN on the movies.

4

NICKELODEONS PLUS

AS Brutus observed, when filtered through Wm Shagspe, "There is a tide in the affairs of men that, taken at its flood, leads on to fortune."

When William Fox caught that tide on Brooklyn's Broadway in 1904, he hoped for the best, but he certainly had no idea that it would catapult him into a fortune of three hundred million dollars. Nor had he the philosophy of James Russell Lowell, who commented that, while "there is a tide in the affairs of men, there is no gulf stream setting forever in one direction."

As he was swept, as on a surfboard, to the very crest of the waves, Fox crashed from his peak onto the rugged shore and, bruised and beaten, set out again to catch the tide of victory.

Always a loner, William Fox felt cramped with partners, although at the turn of the century he pooled his theatres with those of B. S. Moss and Sol Brill in Fox, Moss and Brill. This exhibition partnership brought some strength in dealing with the patents monopoly that supplied practically all of the one- and two-reel films licensed through the General Film Company. Before that, Fox had been operating modestly from a desk at 24 Union Square, over which he made deals for booking films into the Dewey and City Theatres on Fourteenth Street, the Star at Lexington and 104th Street and the Gotham on 125th Street, in addition to his theatres in Brooklyn.

But before long, the bonds of partnership advantage were chafing, and this association was dissolved, with Moss joining Adolph Zukor in the operation of his theatres.

As an independent, Fox continued to acquire leases on more theatres until he could afford to build his own. He soon decided that the family trade was more important than the fast bucks that could be made from blatant sex pictures, and when he took a lease on the Gayety, an old burlesque house at 194 Grand Street in Brooklyn, he had it fumigated and painted. He renamed it The Comedy.

"I catered to the family trade and made the discovery that the greatest existing enemy of the saloon and the dive is the motion picture theatre. As proof positive of this, the many saloons in the vicinity of my theatres found the business so unprofitable that they closed their doors, so that, unwittingly, I became a reformer," Fox declared.

Sometimes there was good money to be made in reform, and Fox had ten profitable weeks presenting on his stages the Kansas Katastrophe Carry Nation, as she told of her drunken husband who had died of alcoholism and warned her listeners about the demon rum. She was against tobacco too, and refused to go on with her act when Fox came backstage one night smoking a cigar. Since he loved cigars it was a considerable wrench for him to lay off the weed, but he promised, and she carried on for ten weeks at $3,000 a week, which was a good deal for both of them. She also picked up some extra money selling miniature hatchets, for she was fresh from her hatchetations on the mirrors and windows of the ornate Carey House in Wichita and in other "blind pigs" in Kansas, which had long had state prohibition with the usual political payoffs.

Winfield Sheehan, who sometimes relaxed at Jack's all-night bar on Sixth Avenue near 43rd Street, agreed with Fox about saloons:

"Motion pictures whenever they came in contact with the saloon put the saloon out of business because they provide better entertainment for less money and because a man can take his entire family to a motion picture theatre twice a week for a smaller amount than would be required for his personal amusement in a café for an evening. Because motion pictures are the best amusement for the general public and because they are conveniently located, a man who wants to forget his worries will naturally turn to the motion picture house where before his feet sought the brass rail."

(Saturday nights in the New York suburbs and elsewhere these days the admission price is $2.50, which means ten bucks is shot for a family of four, plus popcorn for the kids at 35 cents a carton and whatever other candies and hot dogs are needed to fuel the youngsters. No wonder pop would often rather curl up with old movies on TV, washed down with the beer you choose when you're having more than one.)

To get programs that would hold his audiences for an hour, Fox kept urging Kalem and Selig and Vitagraph and the others to make longer pictures, but the Motion Pictures Patents Company told them not to rock the boat, and they kept right on making only short subjects. As far back as 1908 Fox began his first lawsuit against the patents trust, but there were four years of litigation before he got results.

In 1910 he leased the Old Academy of Music at Fourteenth Street and Irving Place, which had been the opera house until the Metropolitan Opera building was built in 1883. He tried everything: stock, operettas, vaudeville, films. Nothing paid off, and he was about to close with a loss of $380,000 when the Boston owners of the property gave him a scaled-down lease that enabled him to continue, and a decade later to be the host to His Royal Highness the Prince of Wales on his 1921 visit.

Being a smart showman, Fox produced for Wallis Simpson's subsequent husband a gilded chair in which his grandfather had sat when Edward VII was entertained at the opera house. For this royal occasion Fox served up a program of vaudeville and films, including a film short called *The Yellow Dog Catcher,* at which the man who would become Edward VIII and then the Duke of Windsor laughed until he cried. "This is the first bit of relief I have had since I arrived," the prince told Fox. "Now let me stay," was his reaction when his host reminded him that his time was up on the schedule that the British Embassy had for him.

With the Academy, Fox felt that he had arrived. "The first theatre had 146 chairs. It was strictly a commercial proposition. I was looking for an outlet for my business acumen which hadn't found sufficient expression in the cloth examining and shrinking business.

"I gradually acquired a chain of twenty-five theatres

and during this period the commercial element was still uppermost. But as I became established and expanded my business, and life was no longer merely a battle to survive, my thoughts changed. I reached the period in 1912 or 1913 when I found myself with $500,000 in cash that I wanted to invest and I realized that there was a great deal more in life than just making money. What concerned me far more was to make a name that would stand for the finest in entertainment the world over.

"I strove to provide more luxurious theatres than before and to refine the entertainment that we presented. I would not allow anything on the stage or screen that I was unwilling to have my wife and daughters see. Many a picture that I had contracted for and would have to pay for whether I used it or not, was shelved on this account. You see, the popular entertainment at this time was little above the crude burlesque stage, which had been all right for men, but now our audiences were made up of men and women too."

In 1913 Fox expanded his Greater New York Film Rental Company into the Box Office Attractions Company and began producing longer films not only in New York and New Jersey but also in California. Mrs. Fox was usually with him in the evenings after the daughters had been put to bed, telling him about novels she had read and suggesting ideas for pictures. Out of this Mom and Pop collaboration came one of their most amazing financial successes and the longest run on Broadway, except for the D. W. Griffith spectaculars.

They had heard an actor reciting Will Carleton's narrative poem "Over the Hill to the Poorhouse" and noted how he held audiences entranced not only with his elocution but with the message that perhaps they were neglecting their aging parents.

Just at this time a seventy-five-year-old man, broken in health, had appealed to Mrs. Fox for help and she was so touched by his lonely homelessness that she asked her husband to call his predicament to the attention of Jacob Schiff, known for his good works. When Schiff had the man investigated he discovered that he had four sons and two daughters, some of them well-heeled, and Schiff gave their names and addresses to the embarrassed vaudeville magnate.

Mrs. Fox was so annoyed that she wrote to each of them, inviting them to the Fox residence at 316 West 91st Street one evening. Perhaps out of curiosity they all came, and she told them the anonymous story of a sick old man who had appealed to her for help. One daughter, who had recently lost her husband, burst into tears and said that of course she wanted her father to come and live with her. Before they left Mrs. Fox had got them all to agree to send her money every month for the care of ole dad.

Out of these incidents and the Will Carleton poem, Mr. and Mrs. Fox worked out the story in sentimental action, without a star and without a script, and assigned Harry Millarde to direct as they ad-libbed.

"The director came to me every morning and I recited the scenes that he would photograph that day," Fox told Upton Sinclair. "Many times while the story was in progress he insisted that the material he had finished could not possibly make a motion picture."

"When it was finished," Upton Sinclair explains, "it was very sad and sentimental. It was in ten reels, and nobody liked it as it preached a sermon. WF determined at least to give it a trial. It so happened that he had a lease on the Astor Theatre in New York; the lease was to expire in five days, and the picture that was showing there was not very good. WF decided that since he had to pay for the theatre anyway, he would put in 'Over the Hill' for five days and see what happened."

What happened was a three-million-dollar net profit on an investment of $100,000. The film ran for more than a year on Broadway. This was the biggest film Fox produced at his newly opened plant at 850 Tenth Avenue.

Essentially a New York operator, William Fox made his first tentative entry into southern California in 1914, where he rented a big barn opposite the Mack Sennett Studios on Edendale Road.

When he saw what continuous sunshine could do to cut costs in picture making, Fox bought twelve and a half acres on both sides of Western Avenue at the Sunset Boulevard intersection, and by building a production plant there made such a contribution to the economy that he was practically acclaimed a native son.

Even as late as 1919, in those smogless days before the captains of industry moved from New England and the Great Lakes to build their smokestacks in California, the Los Angeles Chamber of Commerce was still making its pitch, and in retrospect one wonders why industry did not respond immediately to these advertisements:

"All of the great stars of filmdom have chosen Southern California for their workshops and most of them make their permanent homes here.

"Nowhere has nature prepared so well for the work of the motion picture producer. It is but natural that the people of this section should follow this lead and welcome, as they do, the expansion of motion picture making and take pride in the fact that Los Angeles is the motion picture capital of the world.

"You realize surely the importance in such essentially sensitive production as the making of motion pictures the vital importance of having every member of the organization awake in the morning and start to work in a flood of happy sunshine.

"Cold rain and slushy snow do not tend to the proper mental condition for the best creative work. Environment affects every member of a film producing organization from the stars, directors and camera men to extras and general helpers. Every film man should carefully consider the above bit of psychology. It is important to success.

"No other city in the world offers seashore, mountains, desert and city civilization within an hour of the studios. There is no cessation of the growing season. Gardens and orchards can be filmed twelve months of the year. Snow scenes may be had within a few miles.

"Cheap electric power is available in any quantity. We can assure you that Southern California is the most ideal city for producing films. The light at eight in the morning is as strong as that at ten anywhere else."

Mission accomplished, the Los Angeles Chamber of Commerce has now stopped advertising, and it wishes the population explosion would peter out. But every day about a thousand people arrive to make their homes in Los Angeles County. They come even as older residents leave.

His tonsils stinging and his boiling point at a new low, Frank Sinatra, in November, 1968, announced that he was selling for $350,000 his estate in smoggy Bel Air (il n'y a pas de bel air là-bas) and was making his permanent residence in his Palm Springs enclave.

"When I have to do records and films I'll take an air-conditioned suite in a Beverly Hills hotel, and get out of the smog as soon as possible."

FADE OUT on Frankie, in his own private plane, jetting over the San Jacinto mountains into the clean desert air.

5

THE MAN WHO KILLED THE
MOVIE TRUST

They can conquer who believe they can.

—JOHN DRYDEN

THE only man in show business who twice won his
patent arguments in appeals to the highest courts,
William Fox dared to challenge monopoly both in silent
pictures and in sound, and it was because of his smashing
victory over the Motion Pictures Patents Company in 1912
that we today have freedom of the screen.

His Tri-Ergon patent triumph two decades later was a
temporary one in 1932 and 1933, but his stupendous victory in 1912 was forever.

Up until that time all patents on motion picture inventions in France, England and the United States had
been pooled and claimed by a tough character named
Jeremiah J. Kennedy. This enforcer had brought together
the warring Edison and Biograph factions in an agreement signed December 18, 1908, precipitated by a decision by Judge Christian Kohlsaat who, on October 24,
1907, in the Federal District Court of Chicago, ruled that
Edison patents had been infringed in the making of a
film by William N. Selig.

At that time the Edison licensees included Vitagraph, Lubin, Essanay, Pathé, Kalem and Melies; and Biograph controlled the pioneering technical developments of Mutascope, Robert W. Paul, Thomas Armat, the Lathams and the three Lumieres.

William Fox, out of self-interest for the programming of his theatres, had long campaigned for longer pictures, but Boss Kennedy ruled that one-reelers and two-reelers, with the price of the film rental dictated by him at twelve cents a foot, were the only permissible and authorized product. In theatres that were charging ten and fifteen cents admission, and even, with vaudeville acts, a quarter, Kennedy enforced his nickelodeon thinking. Just to be independent, Fox called his nickelodeons nickelettes or nicklets.

Kennedy controlled every detail of production and exhibition, and warned producers that they must not pay more than $62.50 for any story and must not, under penalty of license revocation, mention any actor or director or writer on film or in advertising.

As the marketing agency for Motion Pictures Patents Company, Kennedy incorporated in New Jersey in February, 1910, the General Film Company, which by July, 1912, had acquired control of the sixty-seven principal film exchanges supplying pictures to 12,869 theatres in the United States.

The only important film exchange that this monopoly did not own was Box Office Attractions Company, which William Fox had expanded from his Greater New York Film Rental Company, and Kennedy was trying to find an angle to liquidate the independent Fox. It came when Fox advertised that he would buy for distribution any available feature-length pictures. This looked like a challenge to the shorts that General Film Company allowed him to distribute.

Kennedy sent for Fox and offered to buy out his Box Office Attractions. Fox asked $750,000; Kennedy said it was exorbitant. When Fox refused to lower his asking price, Kennedy canceled his license, the revocation arriving in the mail the next day. That did it.

Fox had as a partner in his lease on the Dewey Theatre on 14th Street an astute lawyer named Gustavus A. Rogers, older brother of Saul E. Rogers, who later was general counsel for Fox for two decades. The elder Rogers, acting under the Sherman Anti-Trust laws enacted during the Theodore Roosevelt Administration, brought evidence of monopolistic practices to the attention of the Department of Justice and urged the attorney general to break up the patents trust.

Rogers also brought suit in the New York Supreme Court against General Film Company for common law conspiracy, asking for an injunction and triple damages. While the case was pending in the Court of Appeals, highest New York tribunal, Kennedy realized that he was licked, and sent Walter Irwin to arrange an out-of-court settlement. In addition to withdrawing all restraints against Fox by the Motion Pictures Patents Company, General Film Company paid him $350,000. It was a glorious victory for the thirty-three-year-old challenger, and it marked the end of General Film Company, which was buried under judgments totaling more than $25,-000,000. One of its chief liquidators was Sidney R. Kent who, two decades later, was to become president of Fox Film Corporation.

Not only because he was a fighter and a gambler but because of his Tammany connections, Fox had been practically forced into a position of leadership among exhibitors. His Dewey Theatre was owned by Big Tim Sullivan, as powerful a sachem as Tammany ever produced and a politician who gladly endorsed notes for Fox and others, who were thus welded into his Democratic organization.

But there were reformers in those old days of the movies, and in June, 1907, arcades and nickel shows had acquired such a bad reputation that Police Commissioner Bingham recommended to Mayor George B. McClellan that they be wiped out by cancellation of their licenses. From coast to coast, and especially in Chicago where "the world's greatest newspaper" was campaigning against the crime and immorality induced by locally produced films (and where Louella Parsons sold her first story to Essanay), movies were under attack.

Among New York exhibitors the 1908 Yule will always be remembered as Black Christmas, for at midnight December 24th, all the nickel shows in the city were closed by Mayor George B. McClellan, as unclean and immoral places of amusement. After this midnight tragedy Marcus Loew and Adolph Zukor joined with every other operator of nickelodeons and elected Fox to be their leader in their fight to save their golden nickel mines.

Christmas was no holiday for Gustavus Rogers as he worked all night preparing four injunctions against the license commissioners who had closed the peepshow arcades and projection parlors. When they reopened for business in a few days, the Zukors and the Loews and the Laemmles and the Foxes all made New Year's resolutions to clean up their establishments and cultivate the family trade with wholesome pictures.

6

THE CORPORATE FOX

Get place and wealth, if possible, with grace; If not, by any means, get wealth and place.

—HORACE

WITH the February 1, 1915, incorporation in New York of Fox Film Corporation, the 1916 opening of the Sunset and Western studios in Hollywood and the dedication in 1919 of the four floors of the head office and laboratory at 850 Tenth Avenue, New York, William Fox had created, almost single-handedly, the facilities for a world-wide organization of production, distribution and exhibition.

From the command post in his cathedral-like office, with its stained glass windows, Fox telephoned his vice president in Hollywood.

"Pack your bags and catch the next Chief, Winnie, we're going to Europe."

On March 7, 1919, these two invaders sailed for the continent, and when they returned two months later they had established offices in Paris, Rome, Berlin, London and Dublin and had engaged managers not only to get their pictures into theatres at maximum rentals, but also to facilitate the filming of Fox News events and to scout

Europe for screen talent and stage shows suitable for picturization.

While they were away the two brothers of Mrs. Fox, Jack and Joe Leo, minded the store, Jack on distribution and Joe on theatres.

Sol Wurtzel, who had been secretary and general assistant to Fox, had been placed in charge of the Hollywood studios, and was a conscientious superintendent who knew everything that was going on, and who developed an amazing faculty for analyzing the daily rushes screened every morning as a record of each director's previous day's work.

Sol had a compulsive wink in one eye that could be disconcerting. When the lights came on in the projection room the first time I looked at rushes with him, Sol winked at me and I winked back, unaware of his tic.

"Which was the best take in that last batch?" he demanded.

"Three," I said, fast on the uptake, although I hadn't been paying much attention to details beyond my responsibility.

"Wrong," he announced, "that's the scene where there's a bad shadow on the girl's face. Six is the only good take."

From then on I paid more attention to the rushes.

While Fox was in Hollywood in 1916 he spoke to a cowboy, in full regalia, who camped at the studio gate every morning and evening. The cowboy told Fox that he was the sole support of six trained horses, and Fox agreed to pay him $350 a week for horses and rider. This transaction launched the fabulous career of Tom Mix, first and biggest of the Western stars. Mix was an authentic Westerner, having been U.S. Marshal in Oklahoma in 1910 when a Selig director cast him for a real life part in a one reeler entitled *Ranch Life in the Great Southwest*. As a boy he had been in actual combat in Cuba and the Philippines, which came naturally since his father was a captain in the 7th U.S. Cavalry. With this background he brought more realism to Fox pictures than William S. Hart brought from the Broadway stage to Artcraft and Zukor. Bill Hart became such an enormous success that he had to quit work in 1922 because income taxes were eating up his profits.

Fox stabled the horses at the Sunset and Western studios and began making action pictures, with Mix doing his own spectacular jumping from the cliffs. As he developed into an international hero, Tom Mix changed hardly at all in features such as *Two Gun Man, Coming of the Law, Fighting for Gold* and *Fame and Fortune*. When Mix retired after a decade, both three-letter words had made a fortune.

On the distaff side the biggest star was Theodosia Goodman. She had been an unknown, the daughter of a Cincinnati tailor, when she was tested and hired for $75 a week to play the lead in *A Fool There Was*, inspired by Rudyard Kipling's poem about a rag and a bone and a hank of hair. In exotic makeup and Arabian dress, she was transformed on and off screen to Theda Bara, which is Arab spelled backwards. Her subtitled "Kiss me, my fool" became the rallying cry that united the amateur sheiks of the world. She also enriched the English language with a new meaning for the noun and verb "vamp," defined by Webster as "one who uses her charm or wiles to gain admiration and attention from the opposite sex."

From the time Fox hired her in January, 1916, until she quit in 1919, she made forty pictures, and Fox created a veritable Theda Bara industry, turning out a picture every month. She reached her peak with the battle of the *Carmens*. By any standards Geraldine Farrar, the Metropolitan opera star, had more beauty, talent and class than Theodosia, and Jesse L. Lasky provided a special private railroad car to transport the diva Farrar to Hollywood for ten weeks at $2,500 a week.

By that time Theda Bara was being paid $4,000 a week, as they knocked out their rival versions of the story by Prosper Mérimée only a few blocks apart on Sunset Boulevard. Whatever the artistic merits of the pictures, both released in November, 1915, the financial victory was scored by the established movie star, for Farrar, after all, could not sing in silent films. Both girls smoked cigarettes, which was daring for the ladies of that era.

The female form, exposed at the turn of the century only in boudoirs, bawdy houses and museums, popped out larger than life in theatres playing *The Daughter of the Gods,* a spectacular feature directed by Herbert Brenon in Jamaica. In this film Annette Kellerman was revealed in a one-piece bathing suit, covered from neck to toes. Among the bikinis of today it would be quaint, but then it was daring, as were the bare knees that Mack Sennett and Keystone commercialized in their bathing beauty comedies.

After Stanford White, architect of the original Madison Square Garden, was shot and killed by the jealous Harry Thaw, the object of their affections became a celebrity, and Fox starred Evelyn Nesbit in such titles as *Fallen Idol* and *The Woman Who Gave.*

One midnight Fox sat at his kitchen table eating one of the delicacies that his Eve had prepared for him.

"How do you spell gefulte fish?" he demanded.

"Spell it? Don't I have enough trouble making it? I'll buy a Yiddish dictionary and find out."

They were accumulating a modest home library as Mrs. Fox used her spare time to read novels, always on the lookout for plots for her husband's expanding production.

In 1917 she read Victor Hugo's classic *Les Miserables* and had trouble pronouncing the names of some of the characters. Here was a big book they could get for nothing, the copyright having expired, and it looked like a bargain, except for the title, which they considered changing to "In the Sewers of Paris." But Hettie Gray Baker advised against changing the title.

Miss Baker was a college girl who had titled some silent pictures so expertly that Fox sent for H. G. Baker and was surprised by her sex and impressed by her charm and talent. She remained at the head office to establish a library and to become the first Fox story editor. She also selected, with attention to both bindings and content, the books for Fox Hall when Will and Eve and Mona and Belle moved from their Manhattan apartment to the luxurious estate adjoining the Woodmere Golf Club.

William Farnum was a tremendous hit in *Les Miserables,* directed in 1918 by Frank Lloyd, who later won many awards for his artistry in talking pictures.

John Ford, with all his accumulated Academy and other awards, made his first big epic for Fox in 1924 when he directed *The Iron Horse,* dramatizing the linking of the first transcontinental rails laid east by Chinamen and west by Irish laborers. His *Four Sons* was acclaimed by critics as one of the great pictures of the late silent era, which also included such memorable attractions as *The Big Parade* from MGM, *All Quiet on the Western Front* from Universal, *The Front Page* from United Artists and *Grass* and *Chang* by Merian Cooper and Ernest Schoedsack for Paramount.

The Fox flow of silents was carried along with such names as June Caprice, Gladys Brockwell, Virginia Pearson and Madge Bellamy, all beauties who were lookers if not talkers for the new sound era.

At the Terminal and American Theatres in Newark, the New Jersey group that had supplied the money for the capitalization of Fox Film Corporation in 1915 watched over their investments, noting the weekend crowds standing in line to buy tickets, and checking on the net earnings, which jumped from over half a million in 1915 and 1917 to $2,660,158 in 1924. In 1925 they suggested that this might be the opportune moment to go public. By that time their initial investment of $400,-000, which they had recouped in two years, had brought them dividends of around $8,000,000.

In 1925 Fox Film Corporation was recapitalized at a million shares, of which only half a million were issued at the beginning. The 900,000 A shares had no votes and Fox had absolute control of the remaining 100,000 B voting shares.

He was always buying and selling theatres, and in 1919 he operated eight in Manhattan, including the Audubon and Crotona which he had built, the Tremont in The Bronx, four in Brooklyn, one in Jamaica, four in New Jersey, one in Connecticut, one in Massachusetts, one in Detroit and four in Denver.

It was the enormous theatre expansion to more than a thousand theatres in 1927 and 1928 that overextended his credit and led to his financial ruin.

7

THE FOX FAMILY

History is merely gossip.

—OSCAR WILDE

THE genetic theory that the first-born acquires a bio-
logic advantage over later babies finds some confirmation in the case of William Fox, eldest of thirteen children.
Six of the babies died, perhaps due to tenement squalor
and poor nutrition, but three sons grew to manhood. The
eldest of these had more than the combined intelligence
of the other two.

Maurice, the youngest, was, when I knew him, a sweet
little man with no pretensions who competently handled
a clerical job in the print department.

Aaron, the middle brother, was a big shot, and why not,
since his brother had made him treasurer of Fox Film
Corporation, treasurer of Fox Theatres Corporation, vice
president of Fox Metropolitan Theatres and director of
various subsidiaries. He was the kind of director who
signs here, with the document—prepared by lawyers—
not revealed to the signatory.

Once, when I was in a West Side barbershop with my
face covered by hot towels, Aaron Fox came in and took
a seat on the shoeshine stand.

"This mug of mine will not sell tickets, so just forget about me,"
William Fox told the author.

William Fox paid William Farnum up to $4,000 a week for a decade after his classic 1914 fight with Tom Santschi in "The Spoilers," by Rex Beach, as filmed in nine reels by Selig. This fine stage actor reached his financial peak in silent films, and worked for only $500 a week in 1934 when he played the railroad president in "The Silver Streak," produced by the author at the RKO studios.

Theda Bara, in 1922, is catapulted into success in "A Fool There Was."

3 Fox presidents who succeeded the founding father

Underwood & Underwood
Harley Clarke
1930–1931

Underwood & Underwood
Edward R. Tinker
1931–1932

Culver Pictures
Sidney R. Kent
1932–1941

Blank & Stoller, Inc.
Saul Rogers, general counsel, who won
spectacular legal battles for William Fox.

Spyros Skouras, president of Twentieth
Century-Fox, 1942 to 1962.

Wide World Photos

William Fox testifying before Senate Committee investigating stock manipulations.

Winfield Sheehan returns in triumph to his desk at the Fox Westwood Studios after being deposed by Chase bankers.

Max Munn Au

Shirley Temple

Janet Gaynor and Charles Farrell

Will Rogers

Westwood studios, looking toward Beverly Hills

"I'm Mr. Fox," he announced to the bootblack. "You take good care of me and I'll take care of you. That's right, give me a good shine. I like my shoes to sparkle. I'm on my way to the Roxy Theater. Have you seen the new show at the Roxy? Great show! You must see it. Just go on over to the theatre and tell the manager that Aaron Fox sent you."

At the Roxy and other Fox theatres the doormen had been alerted to say that a written pass was required.

One day Aaron brought to my office a pretty girl with whom he had lunched and told me he would like me to put her on the publicity payroll. We were expanding so fast that almost anybody who came in could get a job, but since she had no writing experience, no newspaper or magazine background, I hesitated and said I'd let her know when there was an opening. The next time I saw William Fox I asked him about Aaron. He seemed slightly embarrassed but he leveled with me.

"Just use your own judgment. Aaron is an officer of my companies but he has no voice in management."

Among his relatives the Leo boys, Jack and Joe, brothers of Mrs. Fox, were the ones he could always trust. Jack was the executive vice president and second in command, occupying the cathedral-like presidential office when Fox was away from Tenth Avenue.

Joe Leo looked after the expanding chain of Fox theatres, which were under the direction of the old Fox crony John Zanft, a profane diamond in the rough who liked to be called Major, having acquired a commission without the foot-soldiering of Major S. L. Rothafel.

In 1928, when William Fox saw managers and ushers saluting Majors Zanft and Rothafel, he telephoned the editor of the Fox newsreel, Truman Talley, who knew his way around Washington, and asked him to arrange to have Fox commissioned a colonel so that he would rate a salute from his underlings. Only Truman knew what wiles and promises of newsreel coverage were offered, but one day he was able to tell Fox that if he would go to Washington he would be commissioned a colonel.

"Go to Washington to be sworn in? Hell, I'm too busy for that. Let them come to me." And so Fox never rated a formal salute.

His closest companion and habitual golfing partner was Jacob Rubenstein, who lived in an apartment over the boathouse at the yacht landing. Rubenstein was one of the foursome on the history-making day when Fox made his third hole in one, and Rubenstein was injured on the even more memorable day when the Rolls-Royce was wrecked and the chauffeur was killed.

Another frequent visitor at Fox Hall was Albert Greenfield, the Philadelphia real estate wheeler-dealer who was involved in Fox financing, and was present one day in 1930 when money was so desperately needed that the sale of the Tri-Ergon patents was being discussed.

As Fox confided to Upton Sinclair:

"Greenfield took the position that he had been informed again and again that these patents were valueless, and so I might just as well throw them in. There was a time during these sessions that, rather than go on any further, tired as I was, I was ready to surrender these patents. But Mrs. Fox took the position that that could not be; it was these patents that had gotten me into the difficulty; they were the one thing that the Telephone Company wanted, and the one thing the Telephone Company was not going to get. She told Greenfield of the humble way in which we had started; our first year in the $11 a month apartment was the happiest year of her life, and she was willing to go back to such an apartment if she could only take those patents with her.

"Greenfield frankly said that he could not be an impartial friend and advisor in the matter. The securities company, of which he was chairman, was my creditor for $10,000,000, which was almost half the capital of the company, and he had to think about the money. So throughout all this difficulty, Greenfield, who had constant access to my home, was urging that the thing to do was to sell these voting shares and give the Tri-Ergon patents with them.

"I recall one day when he and Harry Sundheim were at my home, and Greenfield was persisting that the transaction be closed, that the Tri-Ergon patents be surrendered. Mrs. Fox was in the doorway, with only a curtain between us, listening to this conversation of Greenfield's. She came into the room and went into a rage of a kind I would never like to see her or anyone in again; it resulted in a terrific expression of frenzy, and she finally dropped to the floor and passed out. For a while I thought she was dead; it took us half an hour to bring her to again."

But by far the most amusing and amazing visitor who had ingratiated himself into the Fox household was the little man with big ideas, Alfred Cleveland Blumenthal, described by an anonymous newspaper writer as "a pint-sized financier in a suit of June-bug green, as restless as a Mexican jumping bean—and not much bigger."

Having no son of her own, Mrs. Fox mothered this mighty midget who called her mother, and defended him one night in 1929 when William Fox woke up screaming in a nightmare, dreaming that Blumy had double-crossed him.

"All the others that you have had faith in may double-cross you, but never Blumy," his wife assured him. But just to make sure, Fox telephoned Blumy in London and asked him to cable a million and a half dollars, the Fox share of the Foxthal commissions in the purchase of a 49 per cent interest in British Gaumont theatres.

Blumenthal promised, but after two trans-Atlantic calls, no money had arrived.

"We have been double-crossed; that was no dream at all," Fox declared. And soon Blumy was sending cables indicating that "he was acting under assignment from the Telephone Company; that he had a mission to perform over there."

As Fox later explained it: "That was the time while Sheehan was in London, having his liver cured; and during one of the telephone calls, Blumenthal said: 'Here is Sheehan sitting alongside me. Do you want to talk to him?' " That sounded strange to me, because if ever two men hated each other, it was Blumenthal and Sheehan. Sheehan was always saying 'He is going to double-cross you.' But now here they were friends, and they came back from England together. Blumenthal had gone in July, in a great hurry, and he and his wife had taken just a couple of suitcases.

"This night when he returned to the Ambassador Hotel, vans stopped and eighteen or twenty trunks came in. I was meeting a new Blumenthal. I naturally felt that the first thing he would do would be to tell me about the things that had transpired. Instead he begged to be excused—he must have dinner, and then he wanted to do some unpacking. He couldn't any longer look me in

the eye. I knew that night clearly that Blumenthal was
no longer for me, but was in the employ either of the
Telephone Company or of Harley Clarke."

This was the situation:

"There was a note due and payable at a bank in Boston,
on a contract which Blumenthal had consummated, and
I didn't want that note to go to protest. This was while
I was ill at home, early in December, and Mrs. Fox,
having heard the whole story, decided to send for the
man who had been calling her 'mother' for so many
years. He came to my sick room, and I asked Blumy to
return the money which belonged to Fox Theatres.
Blumy said he wouldn't do it. Then I asked that he repay
$40,000 of the personal loan. This Blumy said he would
do. When I asked that he lend me $400,000 temporarily,
so that I could meet the note of the bank in Boston,
Blumy refused.

"I did not know that my wife was standing behind the
door, listening to this conversation. But now I heard a
sound behind the door and ran out of the room, and
found my wife standing there with a bottle of vitriol in
her hand. She told me how she had bought this, because
she had become convinced that I was going to be killed
in this terrible struggle, and she did not mean to survive
me. But now, listening to this man, Blumy, and realizing
the extent of his perfidy, she said: 'I am going to blind
him. This dog who has called me mother—if he is going
to destroy my husband, I am going to destroy him.' "

William Fox pushed her into the next room and
locked her in, and then got rid of Blumy.

Fortunately for gracious living, the charmer who had
discovered show business when he was a student at the
University of California was not blinded. Some time

before Blumenthal ever met William Fox, on a visit backstage in San Francisco, George M. Cohan seemingly took a fancy to this brash young man, and he gave Blumy a bit part in *Forty-Five Minutes from Broadway*. But while traveling with the troupe back to New York Blumenthal realized that a future as an actor was too precarious (in 1969 about 80 per cent of the Equity membership was unemployed) and returned to California to go into real estate, where Fox met him and was impressed by his knowledge of California real estate values. From then on this nimble undercover man was the Fox real estate partner in acquisitions involving hundreds of millions of dollars.

Blumy adjusted easily to luxury and after he married the Ziegfeld showgirl Peggy Fears (whom I knew casually in my Greenwich Village days) they had a luxurious estate in Larchmont, New York. An occasional weekend guest was His Honor the Mayor, James J. Walker, then living in sin with Betty Compton, while the plump Mrs. Walker fumed and reprised the song that her talented husband had written: "Will You Love Me in December as You Do in May?"

One weekend when his host annoyed him, the mayor threatened, "If you're not good, Blumy, I'm going to spank you and send you back to school."

For more than a decade later Blumy's wife spanked him with alimony litigation, but he was in Mexico partnered with Miguel Alemán, president of Mexico, in real estate developments at Acapulco. He was thus immune from judgments by the ex-Mrs. Blumenthal and the United States Collector of Internal Revenue. In 1957, age seventy, he died broke.

In this "era of wonderful nonsense," as Westbrook

Pegler has called it, melodrama kept recurring in life's shop window at Fox Hall. In November, 1934, the two Fox grandsons were threatened with kidnapping by an extortionist who managed to spell "money" and "dollars" each five different ways in his note demanding five million dollars from Mrs. William Fox. The Nassau County police flushed out a thirty-five-year-old chauffeur named Maurice Monnier. When Assistant United States Attorney James G. Scileppi asked him, "How do you spell money?" he replied, "I spell it different ways when I'm excited." He was sent to the penitentiary.

One day in the summer of 1939 a summons was nailed to the locked door of Fox Hall on the complaint of Mrs. Aaron Fox that she was being deprived of her husband. She claimed that William Fox had locked up her Aaron in a sanitarium in Hartford, Connecticut, to keep him from testifying in a Senate investigation on stock manipulations. Whatever the facts may have been, the Probate Court awarded her the custody of their two children, one of them named William Fox 2nd. On his release from the retreat July 28, 1932, Aaron was charged with abandoning his two children.

He had further embarrassed his brother that summer by grandly announcing that he had organized in Delaware the Aaron Fox Film Corporation with a capitalization of ten million dollars. William, who had agreed to stay out of film business until 1935, issued a disclaimer of any connection with the project; and even the most gullible of speculators were not buying that one. Poor big shot Aaron!

8

MONEY BAGS

He knew that there was only one reality in this world—Money.

—LION FEUCHTWANGER

IN his inexorable scaling of the heights any man who reaches the top can look back at ambitions crushed and egos wounded. Whether he be Sammy Glick or William Fox, he has magnificently earned his hatred. With more compulsive drive than furriers Loew or Zukor, or glove salesman Goldfish, Fox slashed ahead with that shrewd ruthlessness which they practiced and called *chutzpah*.

"Never, I don't want you associating with that crook," declared the matriarchal Mrs. Einfeld in The Bronx when husband Richard was offered a partnership with Fox in a new theatre if he would put his savings into the venture. But her son, then in high school, later student at Columbia University, went to work for Vitagraph in 1920, switched to First National and for a dozen years, until he retired in 1962, with a pension of $1,500 a week, S. Charles Einfeld was vice president in charge of advertising and publicity for Twentieth Century-Fox Film Corporation.

As William Fox pyramided his projects and wheeled

and dealed, his frenzied up and at 'em drive made fortunes for some, like the New Jersey McCarters, Kusers and Usars, but earned trouble and bitter enmities for others, like Sol Brill, who finally got back his $50,000 loan, but not the stock bonus which he said he had been promised in the new Fox Film incorporation.

At the end of the silent era, things were going so well for Mr. and Mrs. Fox that they spent the winter months at Palm Beach, Florida, and Fox inevitably had a whirl at Bradley's, the impeccable gambling establishment where gentlemen could match their wits and hunches against roulette croupiers and dealers in evening clothes.

Whether he wore his usual white socks or dressed suitably for the occasion, William Fox was welcomed by Colonel Edward Riley Bradley, despite his selectivity, for Fox was certainly in the chips, and the odds were always with the house. One night when luck ran against him he wrote a check for $125,000. But, as he tossed in his bed, with memories of how he had been tricked by a goyim slicker in buying his first nickelette, he decided to stop payment on his check; and Colonel Bradley, who prided himself on running an honest establishment, was outraged.

It was the unforgivable sin, something just not done in the Palm Beach of Addison Mizner, son of a bishop. Only a cad would welsh at Bradley's, and the word was soon passed in New York and Hollywood that Fox was not a man to be trusted.

Some years later Fox was trapped at a table in the Waldorf-Astoria Hotel, where a Jewish charity was raising money in one of those hundred-dollar-a-plate dinners. As the campaign manager exhorted contributions and men of substance were giving aid to the worthy enterprise, the spotlight fell on Fox, who rose and pledged $150,000. Ovation!

Later, when the chairman tried to collect, the pledge was brushed aside. Judge Joseph Proskauer, who was the responsible head of the charity, never forgave Fox for his failure to make good on his pledge.

Since Fox was then a public figure with world-wide interests, employing more than 25,000 people, Saul E. Rogers, his old friend and general counsel, spoke to the president of Fox Films and Fox Theatres about his poor public image.

"If your word is no good, how can you expect people to trust you?" asked one of the few men who dared speak to him so frankly. "Outside of your family and your golfing companions, you have very few real friends," he told him.

With the arrogance of the railroading Vanderbilt who earlier had snorted "The public be damned," William Fox replied:

"What do I need friends for when I am sitting on my money bags?"

9

RELUCTANT PIONEER

Speech is civilization itself.

—THOMAS MANN

WITH all his luck, good and bad, William Fox took a chance in 1926 on a process for photographing sound as light, which General Electric and Western Electric and Radio Corporation of America had rejected, and shot to the top with the system of sound-on-film photography that is in general use today.

Fox Movietone knocked out the Vitaphone film-cum-records system which a year earlier had made a fortune for the brothers Warner and Al Jolson with the novelty of *The Jazz Singer*, first shown to the public at the Warner Theatre on Broadway, New York, October 6, 1927.

But after Fox had acquired these sound patents from Theodore Case to develop the Fox-Case Movietone vari-able-density recording system, he got cold feet, according to Courtland Smith, general manager of the Fox-Case Corporation when it was established in August, 1928, and three times ordered Smith to suspend operations.

It is on the record, and nobody can take away the credit, that it was Smith who sent his friend John Joy, adjusting the old school tie, to see Earl I. Sponable, whom Joy had known as a chemistry student at Cornell. What Joy saw and heard at the Case Research Laboratory at Auburn, New York, on March 19, 1926, so impressed him that Smith sold the idea to Fox and arranged a series of demonstrations that convinced Fox that he should finance the developments that completely revolutionized motion pictures.

Sponable, co-inventor with Case of the sound system, was from 1948 to 1950 president of the Society of Motion Picture Engineers, and has compiled a comprehensive record of sound researches, published as a Bulletin of the Society in April and May, 1947. As Sponable explains:

"From the earliest days of motion pictures, inventors had worked on devices to make it possible for them to talk. All had failed dismally, for the problem was serious and difficult. Theodore W. Case had been experimenting since 1911 with lights in order to photograph sound on film. He began while at Yale. The problem was to find substances extremely sensitive to light.

"During the war we gave up our experiments and invented a secret system whereby infra-red light rays could be used for the transmission of signals between ships. Convoys were kept in line by means of this. After the war we returned to Auburn, and work progressed to the point where we perfected an AEO light which was so sensitive to light vibrations that tiny lines of sound could be photographed on motion picture film."

It was a close-up of a canary bird singing, demonstrated to Fox in Parlor B in the newsreel studio at 54th Street and Tenth Avenue, that finally convinced Fox that sound on film really worked. Present on that historic occasion were inventors Case and Sponable, finders Smith and

Joy, and Jack Leo, who had nursed along the sound installations while Fox was in California.

When the house lights came up in the projection room, all eyes were on Fox. He was incredulous. He could not believe what his eyes and ears were telling him. Smith and Sponable have each given me their separate accounts or I would not believe the Fox reaction. Always suspicious, he now actually thought that there was ventriloquism, or some form of trickery. And of course there was: a decade of electronic trickery.

Fox asked that his projection room at Fox Hall be equipped, and the next demonstration was at his home in Woodmere, where he knew that there was no ventriloquist in the projection booth.

Now that he had sound on film, Fox did not know what to do with it, according to Sponable.

"The only thing he could think of in 1926 was to use Movietone as a ballyhoo on the Atlantic City boardwalk to get people in to see vaudeville and programs of silent pictures," Sponable told me, and I was incredulous because when I first met Fox a year later his soaring imagination and enthusiasm for Movietone knew no limits.

"Fox with his Movietone could have been ahead of Vitaphone if Fox had let us go ahead with theatre demonstrations," Sponable revealed, "but he kept me doing tests at the 54th Street studio. I made tests of Gertrude Lawrence, Beatrice Lillie, Raquel Meller, Ben Bernie, Chick Sale, and others.

"While I was testing Harry Lauder, who did not trust Fox, the singer stopped in the middle of a refrain of 'Roamin' in the Gloamin' to announce 'This is a tist.'

"The canny Scot did not realize that we could easily

have edited out his disclaimer if we had wanted to show this film in a theatre."

The first theatre demonstration of Movietone was May 2, 1926, at the Nemo Theatre, 110th Street and Broadway, New York City. Courtland Smith, who was a brother-in-law of Arthur Brisbane, featured editorial thinker for William Randolph Hearst, took it from there, technically and promotionally, and Sponable is on record as saying that "the industry is greatly indebted to Courtland Smith for his foresight and aggressiveness in hastening the commercialization of sound-on-film. He did more than anyone else to convince the doubting Thomases of the business that the days of silent film were numbered. He was instrumental in starting and developing Movietone News and later the Newsreel Theatre."

Smith told me that in the first weeks of these demonstrations Adolph Zukor asked Fox if he could see what was going on, and Fox told Smith to show him everything. After the screening, Zukor said: "I told you that you couldn't do it." Smith later took Jesse L. Lasky to a screening of shorts at the Gaiety Theatre on Broadway, and Lasky was most enthusiastic. Here was the same reaction I had discovered with Magnascope: Zukor the businessman intent on preserving the status quo and Lasky the partner with creative imagination who saw the dramatic potentials. More than a decade later, when Paramount technicians had developed their own wide screen process and were demonstrating VistaVision at the Paramount Theatre on Broadway, Zukor sat in the last row of the orchestra and could not see the top of the big picture because of the balcony overhang. "No good," he announced, in a monotonous replay of his reaction to Magnascope.

If Fox, as Smith says, ordered sound work stopped three times, then it must have been connivance on Smith's part that kept research going and equipment building until the inevitability of sound got through to General Manager Sheehan, who resented the upstart activities of General Manager Smith. At that time Fox was so busy buying theatres and cooking up deals with Blumenthal that I did not hear from him for months, and it may be that Smith let one commitment after another pile up so that there was no stopping the momentum of Movietone.

As fast as sound cameras could be built and sound technicians trained to work with cameramen, new sequences were put on film. On January 21, 1927, at the Sam H. Harris Theatre in New York, the public heard the first songs by Raquel Meller as a prelude to the opening of the nondialogue picture *What Price Glory*. On October 28th the first all-sound newsreel was heard at the Roxy Theatre, consisting of the real sounds and sights of Niagara Falls; the romance of the iron horse, with snorting steam; the Army-Navy football game at Yale Bowl; and some whooping rodeo performers.

Smith produced the first weekly issue of Fox Movietone News on December 3, 1927, and theatre demand was such that it was increased to two regular issues each week in October, 1928, and three weekly issues in December. By then the four competing newsreels, Pathé, Paramount, Universal and Hearst-MGM, were just getting sound cameras into London and Paris, and Fox was so far ahead in world coverage that the competition never caught up.

My younger brother Earl was a factor in this global advantage. He had been handling theatre and travel advertising for the *New York Post,* and unknown to me, with exactly the right timing, called on Smith and asked

him why he didn't have sound cameras in the Orient.
Smith was outraged at his brashness, but when Earl told
him that the only cost would be his salary, because he
could arrange free round-the-world transportation with
one of the steamship lines, Smith hired him. He did not
know anything about directing sound pictures but he had
six weeks to learn before the *Empress of Australia* sailed
on a Canadian Pacific round-the-world cruise, launching
shipboard romance and matrimony for him and a career of
high living, with unlimited expense accounts, for a
quarter of a century.

At every port the sound man, cameraman and director
shipped back to Smith their exotic world harvest:
Christmas bells in Bethlehem, New Year's Eve in Cairo,
untouchables and Maharajahs in India, temple bells on
the road to Mandalay, native dancers in Fiji and Samoa
and the Emperor of Japan in a parade below the camera
stand—an insult to His Majesty for which my brother
was deported from Japan—for nobody, and certainly not
an American newsreel crew, is higher than The Son of
Heaven.

When the conquering heroes returned, Smith sent them
to northern Europe, where they produced a full house:
three kings in Scandinavia and two queens in Belgium
and The Netherlands. Again my brother insulted royalty
in the land of his ancestors, and was deported to Norway
until he could apologize in writing to the King of
Sweden for smoking a cigarette in his presence during
the filming of outdoor gymnastics.

In Spain, King Alfonso XIII had been the first reigning
monarch to speak for Fox Movietone, but the short that
created the biggest world impact was that of George
Bernard Shaw, who directed the crew as he made his
audio-visual debut on film.

The original sound recording equipment cost $25,000 per unit and required a one and a half ton truck, but improvements were being made. On a visit to New York in 1927, when Sheehan saw what was being accomplished, he requisitioned one of the newsreel units and shipped it to Hollywood. On a muffled stage he had John Ford direct *Napoleon's Barber,* by Arthur Caesar, and topped the impact of this first dialogue dramatic short by sending the same crew out on the streets of Los Angeles to make the first dialogue picture filmed outdoors, called *The Family Picnic.* With this demonstration that sound-proof stages were not requisite to production, Sheehan sent a crew into Zion National Park to make *In Old Arizona,* which created a sensation when shown at the Roxy Theatre in January, 1930.

Although the public was not aware of these technical details, Harold B. Franklin, the astute operator of Fox West Coast Theatres, took note not only of *In Old Arizona's* box-office prowess but of its production technique: "This film was photographed and recorded outdoors against a sweeping background of natural beauty, and in it sound recording achieved its highest artistic success up to that time. Filmed and recorded right out in the vast open spaces, the scenes and the human voice and all the accompanying sounds were reproduced with a clearness and naturalness that attracted wide attention. The Movie-tone process caught and reproduced with fidelity not only the voices of actors but actually the sounds of the outdoors, the whispering of the wind, the song of the birds. The picture was thus notable in combining the perfected technique of the silent film with the faithful recording of music, dialog and sound."

While Joseph Schenck was still announcing that sound was just a passing fancy, and other producers were debat-

ing whether to use the Fox system or the RCA Photo-
phone variable-area sound track, Warner Brothers abandoned their records-with-film and began making sound-on-
film pictures.

Not only had Smith's judgment been vindicated with
the Case patents, but he also sent his man Joy to Switzerland to investigate some German patents brought to his
attention by F. A. Schroeder. Three German inventors,
Josef Engl, Hans Vogt and Joseph Massole had worked
out a system whereby the space outside the sprocket holes
was used for a sound track, a photoelectric cell, a fly wheel
and a system of laboratory printing, on which they had
obtained eighteen patents between April, 1919, and July,
1923. Again Joy made his recommendations to Smith and
Smith to Fox, who decided to take a personal gamble with
$50,000 for the North American rights, acquired from
Tri-Ergon A. G. of Zurich. After long litigation these
were the patents that the United States Supreme Court
first approved and then, for reasons of public policy, declared not valid.

If Fox had said no to the Tri-Ergon deal he could have
saved millions of dollars in fighting the Radio Corporation
of America and the American Telephone and Telegraph
Company; if he had actually stopped Fox-Case development he would not have owed AT&T and its Western
Electric and Electrical Research Products $15,000,000 for
equipment; if he had not hired Courtland Smith away
from Will Hays and had said no to his Case and Tri-
Ergon proposals, maybe Fox would not have gone into
bankruptcy and prison. But he said yes.

10

MALICE IN WONDERLAND

Society is built upon trust, and trust upon confidence in one another's integrity.

—ROBERT SOUTH

WHO killed Herman Rosenthal at two o'clock in the morning of July 16, 1912?

Was it Gyp the Blood, Dago Frank, Lefty Louie and Whitie Lewis, duped and doped gunmen who confessed, before they were executed, that they were assassins hired by Tammany police and gamblers?

Was it New York Police Lieutenant Charles Becker, who, on July 30, 1915, died in the electric chair at Sing Sing for the murder, protesting "I am sacrificed for my friends"? He had pleaded to no avail with Governor Charles S. Whitman that "I am innocent as you of having murdered Herman Rosenthal or of having counseled, procured or abetted his murder."

Was Becker framed and did he die refusing to squeal on grafters higher up in Tammany?

Big Tim Sullivan, partner of William Fox in his City Theatre and Democratic boss for whom Rosenthal was graft collector?

Rhinelander Waldo, gentleman Police Commissioner?

Winfield R. Sheehan, secretary to the Police Commissioner?

In March, 1930, when William Fox and Sheehan parted in anger and recrimination, Fox made this ghastly accusation to Upton Sinclair:

"Winfield R. Sheehan . . . the same man whom I had picked up in 1912 or 1913 and had rescued from the murder charge they were making against him as Secretary to the Police Commissioner."

At that time Fox had insisted to Waldo that Sheehan had nothing whatever to do with the murder, but they were friends on the make then, and eighteen years later the three-hundred-million-dollar empire they had built was being battled for by rival bankers in a violent and abortive stockholders' meeting of Fox Film Corporation.

All this happened when I was a boy in Kansas City and fifteen years before I knew Sheehan. During the five years that I worked with him, from 1927 to 1932, he treated me with kindness, generosity and consideration, and we were friends, as well as business associates, during times that try men's souls. Loved, feared and hated, he was Dr. Jekyll and Mr. Hyde in Hollywood, New York, London and Paris.

He was between wives when I knew him, having divorced the Ziegfeld beauty Kay Laurel and not yet married the Austrian operatic soprano Maria Jeritza. In Beverly Hills, he employed thirty-three servants in his Mediterranean palace, built around ceilings and doors and grillwork imported from castles in Spain and Italy. In New York he was usually alone in his suite in the Savoy Plaza. With no female to soothe him in the mornings, he used to work off his tensions by walking in Central Park, and I dreaded the occasional summons to walk around the reservoir with him and so be the first to be exposed to whatever might be on his global mind that day. After a night of drinking and thinking and tossing and worrying, his subconscious sometimes dredged up unexpected broodings and revenges that needed ventilation.

Sheehan was a complex character: affable, sentimental, suspicious, cynical, ruthless, and a squat dynamo of energy. His baby-blue eyes popped out from a florid face that was seldom relaxed. An impetuous enlistment in the Spanish-American war matured him in his teens and took him away from his Roman Catholic family in Buffalo and St. Canisius College. A taste of reporting on the *Buffalo Courier* led him to the *New York World,* where from 1902 until 1910 his police court and tenderloin district reporting gave him an insight into how commercialized vice can operate with police protection and become enormously profitable to Tammany politicians and landlords, including the Trinity parish of the Episcopal Church, which owned many houses of prostitution in the area south of 40th Street between Sixth and Eighth Avenues.

A contemporary *Sun* reporter, Samuel Hopkins Adams, has recreated the era and area in his final novel *Tenderloin,* which was adapted into a top Broadway musical in 1960.

When Tammany tried to achieve respectability by appointing Rhinelander Waldo as fire commissioner, Sheehan joined him as secretary, and moved with him in 1911 as secretary to the police commissioner. After District Attorney Charles Whitman exposed police scandals with such courtroom drama that he became governor of New York, Sheehan joined Fox as his secretary. With his industry, skills and political and financial connections, Sheehan was soon vice president and general manager earning up to $130,000 a year during two decades with William Fox, and from $250,000 to $500,000 annually with the bankers who deposed Fox. Before he assumed charge of production he organized domestic and foreign distribution and launched the Fox newsreel, which William Fox, by technical excellence, pushed way ahead of the original competing Pathé News.

In London, Paris and Berlin, Sheehan worked hard, played harder, but something must have gone wrong on a recent trip abroad, and he surprised me one day on a walk around the reservoir by asking my opinion of the Paris managing director, whom I had only met casually at a sales convention. When I told him that he impressed me as being suave, charming and competent, Sheehan said that he seemed to have me fooled too, but that he was really no good.

"Send him a cable when you get back to the office and tell him that he is to leave in thirty days to take charge of our office in Brazil. Sign my name, send me a carbon and tell him that he will have detailed instructions by letter as to how to proceed in Rio de Janeiro."

Since the man had a French wife and children, a home in Paris and a house in the country, and did not speak Portuguese, the adjustments he had to make were hemispheric. But a dozen years later, when Hitler invaded Paris, perhaps it was all for the best, since the deportee was Jewish, and in Brazil he achieved great wealth.

Sheehan loved to play God, as who with great power does not? Discovering new talent was one of his favorite preoccupations, for the Fox studios had few big stars under contract, and were not in the same name league with Metro-Goldwyn-Mayer ("More stars than there are in heaven").

Back in the silent years he had paired Janet Gaynor

with Charles Farrell, and Nick Stuart with Sue Carol. Sue broke up the team by marrying Alan Ladd and, as his business manager, built him up into such a big star that when he died in 1961, Alan Ladd, junior, was ready to take over as a leading man with his mother as manager.

But when the Gaynor-Farrell screen mating paid off with the very first Academy Award to Janet Gaynor for her performance in *Seventh Heaven,* Sheehan was encouraged to manufacture new young stars to his own specifications. In one of our walks in Central Park he told me that he had dreamed up the name Dixie Lee and asked me how I liked it. I said I thought it was short, sweet, memorable and would look good in electric lights, but I am sure that if I had suggested the same name he would have called it trite, corny and regional. Reacting to titles was a game we played, and I never met him by appointment without having lists of five possible movie titles in each of four pockets, sorted out for musicals, melodramas, comedies and Westerns, so that I could make spontaneous suggestions whenever he demanded a new tag for a picture in work.

He said that he wanted a red-headed blues singer to flesh out his Dixie Lee, and told me to run a display ad on the theatre page of the *Daily News* asking blues singers with red hair to audition at the Globe Theatre on Broadway, the famous Dillinger musical house that was then leased by Fox for the showing of hard-ticket pictures.

Some sixty girls showed up—a few with the red hair dye still wet—and sang their blues. I had called in Joe Pincus, eastern casting director, and he and I and the piano player listened and watched as each girl did her song under the harsh stage lights of the Globe, now the Lunt-Fontanne Theatre.

Most of the girls were amateurish, and understandably

nervous. If there was much genuine talent on that stage it eluded us. One little girl seemed to have a youthful flair, and said that she had been in the chorus of *Good News*. When she told me her name was Wilma Wyatt I asked her if she would mind changing it for Hollywood to Dixie Lee. For a hundred dollars a week she said that would be O.K. I signed her up for six months, with annual options up to a thousand dollars a week, and shipped her out to California by Twentieth Century and Chief, which in those early days of sound carried a heavy traffic of players in control of their vocal chords.

In her first picture she had a small part singing with Paul Whiteman's band, and when I got to the studio about six months later, Sheehan told me that she was doing fine, and might develop into a star if she would take voice lessons and not get mixed up with one of the trio of vocalists who had taken a fancy to her. He was drinking too much, Sheehan said, and Sheehan could qualify as an expert, having known his quota of drunks in the old days at Jack's on Sixth Avenue, just off the Tenderloin, where bouncers were expertly trained to propel to the sidewalk anyone carrying too much laughing soup. He had warned the girl to be careful about her Hollywood associates, and insisted that I have a heart-to-heart talk with her, since she was my discovery.

When I asked Dixie Lee about her love life, if any, she took the position that it was really no concern of mine, and I thought her point well taken. "Don't worry about me," she said, and I ignored her from then on. She went right ahead and married Bing Crosby, and became the mother of handsome sons who, in their twenties, married red-headed showgirls singing the blues in Las Vegas.

In show business the direct approach is seldom effective

and sometimes the shortest distance between two points
is the longest way around. In the boom days of Hollywood
studios, casting offices seemed to be operating communications barriers. With producers and directors appealing for
inspired casting, the same old young faces flowed in a
montage of familiarity.

Having produced the first all-talking short, the first
sound film recorded out of doors and the first sound-on-
film feature, Sheehan decided to produce the first all-Negro
picture, and had a script in work called *Hearts in Dixie,*
for a mature male singer. For reasons unclear to me, the
Fox casting office seemed unable to locate a Negro actor
with a fine singing voice. Sheehan telephoned me from
California asking me to get around in Harlem to see what
I could find, but I was too harassed in trying to ride herd
on sixty people in the advertising and publicity department to spend my time in uptown night clubs.

Meanwhile, out in Hollywood, a Negro singer named
Clarence Muse was trying to get through to the casting
directors at the Sunset and Western studios, which were
being used for sound recording while the new Pico
Boulevard stages were under construction. Possibly because he had no agent, he was getting nowhere, and
couldn't get past the guards at the studio gates to see
the director. But Muse persisted, hanging around the
studio gates until one night, around six, as Sheehan was
being driven out into Western Avenue, Muse fell against
the car or the driver brushed against him, or something,
and an annoyed and embarrassed chauffeur stopped to
help a slightly bruised man who identified himself as an
actor who could sing. Sheehan drove him to a hospital
for a checkup, and the next day his magnificent voice was
being tested.

"I had to knock him down to find him," Sheehan told the director, and *Hearts in Dixie* was a 1929 triumph for Clarence Muse.

Theatres south of the Mason-Dixon line refused to play a Negro picture and the film was not a financial success, but this little picture had a profound impact on William Fox, who ran it over and over again at his projection room at Fox Hall and at the head office. (All the other film studios referred to their home offices in New York, but with Fox it was always the head office—phraseology that seemed to me peculiarly appropriate in a dictatorship run by one head man who, alone among all the film magnates, owned more than 50 per cent stock control of all his enterprises.)

I wondered whether, at the peak of his prosperity, this businessman who had little time for social consciousness was becoming interested in the black man's burden. Then I realized that the master of a three-hundred-million-dollar global empire had only two daughters and no son, and that he was probably finding some vicarious satisfaction in this tear-jerker of father love for an only son, sentimentally written by Walter Weems and directed by Paul Sloane to tear your heart out with a block and tackle. When I watched from the projection booth as Fox sat alone running the picture, I felt as if I were snooping on a man's innermost thoughts, which he may never have admitted even to his devoted womenfolk.

Not until after her husband died did Mrs. William Fox acquire a son, by adopting William Taussig Fox, son of her divorced daughter Mona.

In the current Nassau County telephone directory eighteen men named William Fox are listed, so the founding father has his namesakes as well as half a dozen

theatres on Long Island called Fox, now operated by Fox
Eastern Theatres, a division of National General Corporation, which used to be Fox West Coast Theatres.

Ever since Sheehan had been lucky with Janet Gaynor
and Charles Farrell, he had been trying to develop new
young lovers, but his only big stars were a five-year-old
girl and a character actor who twirled a rope, chewed gum
and told jokes. The enchanting Shirley Temple made her
spectacular impact on film business in *Stand Up and
Cheer* in 1934, and for five years her Fox pictures were
among the year's biggest moneymakers, so designated by
the *Motion Picture Herald.*

Will Rogers, who died in an Alaska airplane crash in
1935, was the only other big Fox star. With his daily
syndicated newspaper comments, he was a one-man publicity organization, and gave me a rough time whenever
I tried to get him to write anything for the annual advertising announcement of his upcoming pictures, so that
at deadline I had to imitate his folksy style and write his
blurb myself, dropping the final Gs.

One of Sheehan's discoveries in Europe was Elissa
Landi, royal daughter of the Countess Zenardi Landi,
who insisted that she was the daughter of Her Majesty
the Empress Elizabeth of Austria, who died by an assassin's
hand in 1898. Her royal spouse, the Emperor Francis-
Joseph, King of Hungary, King of Bohemia, lived on
until 1906, refusing to recognize or to legitimatize Elissa
Landi's mother.

By one of those ironies which the Master Dramatist
is always arranging, this new European charmer was
traveling to Hollywood on the same Century and Chief
with Donald E. McIntyre, a Harley Clarke lieutenant,
and, according to William Fox, just another reader of

gas meters. During the disastrous year that Clarke had been president of Fox, McIntyre had done some research for him, and when the Chase Bank sent in Edward R. Tinker to replace Clarke as president, Tinker, who knew little about film business except on consolidated balance sheets, took a firm line and sent McIntyre out to California to straighten out the Fox Film factories.

I have seen bankers arrive from New York to put three different studios in order and install what they conceive to be sound operating practices. After his chairmanship of the Securities and Exchange Commission, Joseph P. Kennedy, father of a small boy who later grew up to be president, was much in demand as a doctor of ailing corporations. The Paramount board of directors, like the French cabinet before DeGaulle (and Balaban) had shifting alliances, and one of these in 1936 issued a five-year contract to John E. Otterson, formerly of AT&T and the Fox trusteeship. To justify getting rid of Otterson, the new directorate hired Kennedy for a fee of $79,000 to make a survey. What he found wrong in studio operations he blamed on Otterson, who had been in charge less than a year and whose first authorized picture had not been finished.

But by eager-beaver efficiency, soon after Otterson had hired me for five years (with annual options) as chairman of the editorial board at the studio, I inadvertently fed the Kennedy investigators with deplorable evidence of Paramount inefficiency. Everybody knows, except bankers, that not all stories stand up in scripting, casting and current events (like the comedy of military high jinks in Honolulu awaiting release when Pearl Harbor was bombed). In twenty years, way back to the merger of Zukor's Famous Players with Jesse L. Lasky, Paramount had accumulated 333 owned and unproduced stories. For the first time since talking pictures, I made an analysis of these plays, novels and originals, and recommended that the studio offer about half of them for sale.

Kennedy read my report and incorporated parts of it into his 15,000-word memorandum to prove the woeful inefficiency of studio operations. Paramount paid me off for the remaining months of my contract, but Otterson's had four years to go, and they paid him around $2,000 a week for not working, which is the kind of work I am still looking for.

When Otterson returned from the studio to his New York office in the Paramount building (across 44th Street from One Astor Plaza) he could not get to his desk, because nobody could find the office key, and the president was locked out of the office to which he reported daily until a legal settlement was made.

But these were mild developments compared to the melodramatics at Fox when the bankers sent out their reader of gas meters to monitor Movietone City.

The McIntyre safari to Hollywood may have been the factual basis for the hilarious novel *Mr. Dayton, Darling,* by Lady Mary Cameron, who was no lady in the sense in which she used the word, but was at that time a story editor for R.K.O.-Radio Pictures.

News of the impending studio reorganization reached Sheehan in time for a nervous breakdown, and he cleaned out his desk and went to San Francisco with two Jesuit priests to comfort him. McIntyre moved into Sheehan's office and began pressing buttons. Lawyers brought contracts, and accountants showed budgets and payrolls. Wherever he turned, McIntyre, of Scotch or north of Ireland ancestry, found the entrenched Sol Wurtzel tribe or the Winnie Sheehan clan. It took considerable inquiry before he located an executive who was neither Catholic nor Jewish, and from whom he might presumably get some objective advice. Harley Clarke was a Christian Scientist, and when McIntyre discovered an assistant story editor of that faith, who had a Midwest background similar to his own, he knew that he had found a man whose judgment he could trust.

About a year previously Sheehan had employed this newspaper man and started him reading new literary material and writing story synopses. By coincidence I traveled west with him as he was beginning his studio assignment. Since he had never been in California previously, he asked me about the studio, and I answered all of his questions in considerable detail. Some of my comments were so absurd that he knew that I was kidding the new boy although I was really trying to help him get off to a right start in a dream factory.

I remember specifically warning him to be nice to Riley the Cop, whom I described as wearing riding togs during his morning horsemanship, luncheon clothes in the Café de Paris, striped pants in the afternoon, tuxedo in the evening but never a policeman's uniform. He had worn uniform back in New York as confidential man in the office of the secretary to the New York police commissioner, and now, as studio director of safety, his salary was bigger than that of the chief of Los Angeles Police. Joseph Riley was a formidable and zealous one-man intelligence service, the studio OGPU, head of Sheehan's secret police.

The new actress, reared in the ways of royalty, was established by McIntyre in the best dressing room suite, and these two novices, who had never been in a studio before, began making policy decisions.

To conserve time, and get on with the housecleaning, it was arranged that the story editor would pick up McIntyre every morning in a chauffeur-driven Lincoln from the studio garage, pending the abolition of this costly facility. The uniformed driver was courteous and menial, for he was Riley the Cop. Shy, naïve and inclined to be an introvert, the story editor had been so intent on the fictional characters in his synopses that he had not identified this real life character.

Every morning, as they drove to work, the new top banana would discuss with the story editor which one of the studio personnel was to be fired that day, or have his contract broken, so that nobody would be making more money than any of the seventy-nine vice presidents of the Chase National Bank. Within the hour Sheehan in San Francisco would have a telephoned report of the proposed improvements for the day, and of the derogation heaped upon him for his stupidity and cupidity. Registered mail the next day brought transcripts of conversations recorded from tapped telephone wires. Not even when he was at the controls in his own florid flesh had Sheehan had such a masterfully detailed account of the studio's daily activity.

After Nathan Burkan, Sheehan's attorney in New York, had studied the slanders of a fortnight and listened to some of the recorded conversations, he conferred with counsel for the Chase National Bank. The integrity and intelligence of his client had been sufficiently maligned, in the opinion of this distinguished attorney, to begin action for criminal libel against McIntyre and his employers, and for damages for breach of contract.

Hurriedly summoned to New York to give an account of his studio management, McIntyre checked in at the Hotel St. Moritz on Central Park South and waited for the call that never came from President Tinker. I was at the studio when Sheehan returned in triumph from San Francisco to his office.

"I've decided to make some changes," he told me, "and one promotion. Better write this down, so you'll get it right. I want Louella Parsons to have this exclusively. Our assistant story editor has been promoted to the newly created post of assistant to the director of safety, who, as you know, has charge of transportation, including garages and stables. In his new post the assistant will have the personal responsibility for cleaning up after the horses."

His bulging blue eyes twinkled.

"Have you got that all down?"

"Yes, Mr. Sheehan."

I telephoned Louella her exclusive.

Back in New York a month later I read in the newspapers that a man named Donald E. McIntyre had jumped or fallen from a window on the twenty-first floor of the Hotel St. Moritz. In his room detectives found a typewritten report of a proposed studio reorganization which nobody at the bank wanted to read.

11

HARVARD UNIVERSITY
PRESENTS WILLIAM FOX

*Time will explain it all. He is a talker, and needs
no questioning before he speaks.*

—EURIPIDES

IN 1927 a Harvard graduate named Joseph P. Kennedy,
who had become so fascinated by the movies and by a
movie star that he personally financed and produced
Queen Kelly, with Erich von Stroheim directing Gloria
Swanson, arranged a series of lectures in the Harvard
Graduate School of Business Administration. Talks were
made in Baker Library by representatives of all the big
companies, including two immigrants who had never
finished grammar school.

Marcus Loew, highly articulate in business arguments
but never much of a speaker, was overcome with emotion
as he confided, "I cannot begin to tell you how it im-
presses me, coming to a great college such as this, to de-
liver a lecture, when I have never even seen the inside of
one before."

But William Fox was unawed by the Ivy Leaguers, and
addressed them with aplomb. His reminiscences and
recollections of his rise to ownership of enterprises employing thousands of people in practically every country

except Russia, and his answers to student questions, reveal a confident global leader unaware of his and Wall Street's impending crash two years later. What follows is Harvard University presenting William Fox:

More than twenty years ago I learned very promptly that I never could earn a livelihood as a speaker, so that the first chance I got some years afterward to go into a profession that did not require any talking but depended entirely on the camera, I took, knowing it was silent. I had really no other choice if I wanted three meals a day.

The picture of today, as men in our organization see it, is not the picture of years ago. Today, the motion picture has a host of admirers. There are still many skeptics, still others who dislike it, and many who hate it, but twenty or twenty-five years ago the hatred was universal. During that period, to have expected to have Harvard agree to have someone meet with its students and tell them something about motion pictures would have been a sacrilege. It was a period when, if a boy was arrested for stealing, his attorney found the most convenient defense to be that he learned to commit this crime because he witnessed motion pictures. If a man was arrested for wife-beating, his lawyer said that he had acquired the habit because he was a regular patron of a motion picture theatre. The newspapers throughout the country, without exception to the rule, were its biggest and staunchest enemies. Whether it was because it was good reading matter or because the populace had no liking for motion pictures or because they recognized the fact that the motion picture was some day destined to be of potential value, and perhaps in a competitive way, I do not know. At any event, the motion picture has since developed the newsreel that from twenty to twenty-five million people a day read in the motion picture theatres. Whatever their motive, there had grown in the hearts of the newspaper publishers a bitter hatred for the motion picture, and that was something that had to be overcome.

The motion picture when it started did not appeal to the native born. He had other forms of recreation and entertainment. The motion picture appealed mainly to the foreign born, who could not speak or understand our tongue, who had no theatre where he could hear his own tongue. He was a Pole, a Russian, a Slav or of some other foreign nationality. He wanted a diversion and found it in the motion picture. It was the money contributed by the foreign born towards the purchase of tickets that enabled the people in the motion picture business at that time to enlarge their scope until the industry grew to such a size that it had a right to expect the respect of the populace of the world. People were skeptical of the motion picture as they were skeptical whether it was right to change from wood to steel in shipbuilding.

The motion picture business went along on that line and against those odds for a number of years until one day some "wise" men in this country decided that the opportunity presented itself to monopolize the motion picture. In those days they had a perfect control of the business. They organized and called their company the Motion Picture Patents Company. No man was allowed to use a motion picture camera unless he received a license from that company. They regulated the wages paid in every branch of the industry. In their judgment, no man who wrote a story and gave his brains to create material for motion pictures was entitled to more than $25 for the finest story that he could write. For those men who were known as directors of motion pictures they established a salary of $50 a week. The highest salary they agreed to pay a performer was $60 a week. They made up their minds that this was not an industry or art but that it was a mechanical occupation and that it required no brains. They controlled the majority of the theatres of the country. They had driven out of business, legally or illegally, every man who had started in this business ten years prior. They either bought him out or drove him out. There were one hundred and twenty of those men, and one hundred and nineteen of them they had driven out or bought out. The only concern that refused to be driven out or bought out was one in which I had an interest, the Greater New York Film Rental Company. We brought the matter to the attention of the federal government, and during the time that William Howard Taft was president and George W. Wickersham was attorney-general they recognized the fact that a great thought was about to be stifled, that a great art was about to die. They saw that it could not be controlled or monopolized, that there ought to be a free field for every free thinking person, and they dissolved that trust and drove those men out of business. That opened the door to the world to enter the motion picture field.

That dissolution invited great brains to write for the screen. The price of the story is no longer measured by its length but by the greatness of it and, instead of $25 for a story, as high as $250,000 is being paid for the right to reproduce a great story in motion pictures. Instead of paying the men who direct motion pictures a uniform scale, the men who direct motion pictures earn all they are capable of earning, depending entirely on their ability, and their salaries range from $100 a week to half a million dollars a year. Men in all walks of life have applied and asked to be of help and aid in the motion picture.

Today there are twenty-five million in this country who are vitally interested in motion pictures, and those who have something to do with the management of that business today have a problem on their hands. That problem can be solved only by the younger generation's taking an active part and being of help in further developing the business. The majority of the men who are in this business are thinking in exactly the same terms as they thought twenty years ago, and what the motion picture industry needs today more than anything else is not the thought of 1907 but the thought of 1927, and that can come only from young America.

The supremacy of motion pictures was not in America twelve or fifteen years ago. It was in England. Today it lies in America. Today, one of the greatest problems confronting England and the British Parliament, and a matter that is being discussed at every session, is how they can bring back the motion picture industry into England, not because of the profit they may earn from the motion pictures that are manufactured and distributed but because of the fact that they charge us with Americanizing the world. They say we have made the Englishman living in London think as we think here in America and they do not want him to think that way. They want him to think their way. They want him to think in the terms of an Englishman. They say that the motion pictures we have presented there and have given to the world have brought us commerce and trade that ordinarily would belong to England. They have taken the motion picture more seriously than we have taken it here. Recently the House of Lords passed an act providing for the subsidizing of English motion picture companies for five or six million dollars or pounds in the hope that they can bring their trade back to England again.

The motion picture has been used for only one purpose up to this time, and that is for entertainment and for spreading the news of the world in the newsreel. That is not the only function it can perform and it is not the only function it will perform. I make the prediction that before the next generation, within twenty years, you will find that the schools of the world will teach not by books but by motion pictures. Mr. Arthur Brisbane, one of the great authorities of this country, has stated again and again that that which is taught to the human being through the eye is everlasting because it makes an indelible record on his brain, while that which is taught through the ear may or may not be remembered, that we distinctly remember everything we see but we do not remember everything we hear.

It is rather odd to find the difference in thought as it makes up the human emotions. One of the greatest motion picture directors, the genius of this age, is a gentleman by the name of Dr. Murnau. He is a German who about two or three years ago made the greatest motion picture of all time called *The Last Laugh*. He conceived the idea that the motion picture must tell its story by picture and not by reading matter and he proceeded to make a motion picture that took two hours to unfold without a single word in titles. The only insert he had in his entire story was a copy of a letter one character had written to another. In other words, the story unfolded itself entirely with the camera. It was a huge success abroad and, although the greatest motion picture of all time, was one of the greatest failures here.

We tried to make a survey and find out why it was a great success in the balance of the world and a failure here and we came to this conclusion. For the benefit of those who have not seen the picture, the story of *The Last Laugh* was written about an old man who was a carriage attendant or door tender in front of a large hotel and wore one of those gorgeous uniforms with gold braid and gold buttons. In Europe, from the time he begins to observe, his dream is to be someone who may wear a uniform. The military uniform, of course, is his first thought, but if he cannot get that, he thinks that probably a letter carrier has the next greatest vocation, particularly in Germany where before the war the average citizen would salute as he passed the letter box with the design of the crown on it. In Germany in particular, every person who wears a uniform, regardless of what his vocation is, considers that that is the greatest honor that can be bestowed on him. And this old man loved his uniform. When he became too old and too feeble to attend the carriages and open the door and lift the trunks off the cars as they pulled up to the hotel, the management decided to make him an attendant in the washroom.

That was the basis of the play and all of Germany wept with this man. Men and women went to see this picture, not once or twice or three times, but as many times as they could possibly spare the time to go and see it, so that they could have a chance to cry about this great character who had been demoted from a man attending a door at a hotel to a man in the washroom. The emotions were perfect for Europe. They were imperfect for America, and they were imperfect in this regard.

A man attending a door in front of a hotel in this country receives a salary, perhaps of $25 a week; he gets very few tips and that is why the management pays him a salary. The ambition of his life is some day to save enough money to be able to buy the washroom privilege, to pay so many thousand dollars a year for the right to be attendant in the washroom where he receives a tip every time you wash your hands. In this country we consider that the man going from door attendant to washroom attendant is promoted. Over there they regard him as demoted.

It was kind of the gentleman who introduced me to tell you that I had just acquired the largest motion picture house in the world. The thrill to me in that is that when I first started, the amount of money that I had enabled me to buy at that time the smallest motion picture house in the world, and the thing that caused me to buy the largest was the fact that I once owned the very smallest. There were not any smaller than that. It had one hundred and forty-six chairs.

The thing that thrilled me the other day was to see the thousands of people who stood in line waiting to go into this new modern Roxy. I distinctly recalled that twenty-four years ago, when I bought this hundred-and-forty-six-seat theatre, the man who sold it to me told me I would do a fine business. He said, "Do not worry about the business—that is all set for you." So we finally opened the door, and not a soul would buy a ticket. I had the $600 that I started with and finally ran it into a bankroll of $1,600, and all of it was in this one thing. I saw beautiful visions of going back and asking for my job, in which the maximum salary I had ever earned before I went into business for myself was $17 a week. I saw visions of again returning to that and leaving this thing that held out the world to me and I wondered what to do and why the thing was not doing business. I was satisfied that it was wonderful. The man who sold me the theater showed me motion pictures in his little studio, and to me they were marvelous. True, the public had not seen them. There was only one motion picture theater in New York itself and there was no other motion picture theatre than this one in Brooklyn, and I could not quite understand how it was possible for anyone to be unwilling to pay a nickel to witness this entertainment. We called it a nickelette.

A man who had fed the lions and the tigers with Barnum and Bailey's show heard that I had made this purchase—he was out of a job, too—and said, "Any time we go in a town and the crowd will not come in, we have a ballyhoo in front of the door to attract the crowd." I said, "What would that cost?" He said, "It depends on what kind you want; I can get you a sword swallower for $2 a night or a fire eater for $3 a night or a coin manipulator for all that he can pick." I asked him to get one of each and to make sure that the other two would watch the coin manipulator. The sword swallower did swallow a sword. I do not know yet how he did it. I suppose it was one of those collapsible things. I thought it was going right through. Soon a crowd gathered, and then he said he would conclude his performance upstairs. It was two flights up, and the crowd followed him up. This seems strange told in 1927, but that was 1903. I remember distinctly, when in the first picture the wind blew through the leaves of the trees, hearing an old fellow say, "They can't fool me, gol dern 'em; I know some one is shaking that screen." Can you imagine such a remark made anywhere today?

After enticing a dozen or more of these audiences a day into this little place, at the conclusion of a week or ten days the hundred and forty-six chairs were not enough to take care of the number of people who were willing to come. We needed no more ballyhoos. The coin manipulator lost his job. He had to go elsewhere. This little bit of a theatre into which I had put $1,600 brought in, in five years, approximately $250,000. In 1927, $250,000 does not seem like a lot of money, but it was an awful lot in 1903. It was that little establishment that made it possible for me to build the organization we now have and it was that method that had to be employed to convince the people of this country ultimately that the motion picture was not just something that might run along but something that would prove worthwhile and something that the nation at large would accept.

QUESTION PERIOD

Question: Do you think that in the large motion picture theatres, like the one you have just bought, they will have a program exclusively of motion pictures, or will there be a tendency toward vaudeville acts and those special things that seem to harmonize with the pictures?

Fox: At the Roxy Theatre the motion picture is about one hour of the two-hour performance. The other hour is devoted to an overture by one hundred and ten of the finest musical artists, probably second only to that which would appear at Carnegie Hall. Then there is a ballet of fifty or seventy-five ballet dancers of the type you would see at the Metropolitan Opera House, and a male chorus of about sixty voices. The fourth is a spectacular number in which over two hundred people are on the stage at one time.

Roxy is the greatest genius we have in motion pictures

from the standpoint of exhibiting, and it is that genius for entertainment that made him famous. If you ever get to New York and see the Roxy I know that you will find the memory of that entertainment to be a lasting one.

Question: You rather look forward to the development of a distinctive art in this kind of a theatre, in which the motion pictures are a part?

Fox: In which the motion pictures are an important part. Although you have this stupendous program in addition to the motion picture, if the motion picture is not good, that part of the program is spoiled and the show cannot be considered a great success.

Question: Do you believe the so-called talking film is going to be very widely used in the future?

Fox: I was going to leave that subject for another gentleman who is coming here, Mr. Warner. I feel he will want to cover that subject. We have an instrument called the movietone, but Mr. Warner seems to be so set on his vitaphone that I would rather leave that subject to him.

As to whether it will be a factor, just imagine professors of this college coming to our studio and delivering lectures on subjects they have studied for years and that they hope to present to this body of students. We photograph the speaker and at the same time on the same celluloid we photograph his voice. That lecture can simultaneously be shown, not only in Harvard, but in all the universities of the world, so that the speaker's voice may be heard in a thousand classrooms at one time.

The movietone or the vitaphone or whatever talking apparatus the public will ultimately adopt will be one of the greatest factors for education that it is possible to conceive. It will take maybe ten or twenty years before it will be recognized as a great educator.

Question: Does your organization make any extensive use of statistics?

Fox: We do.

Question: Have you found such statistics very valuable?

Fox: A man who tries to operate any large business today without having the proper statistics compiled for him and without knowing all the facts and having them before him is groping in the dark. His competitor who uses modern methods will forge ahead of him.

Question: How long did it take you to get $250,000 out of that first theatre?

Fox: I said we made that amount during the first five years. I earned an average of $50,000 a year.

Question: What was your next move?

Fox: Remember this one cost only $1,600, so that every time we got $1,600 more we opened another just like it. Under the law, the maximum number of chairs at that time was two hundred and ninety-nine. The minute you had more than two hundred and ninety-nine seats, you were obliged to build under certain fire regulations and you had to have a modern, fireproof building. We kept investing our money in these two hundred and ninety-nine seat theatres until one day they passed a law permitting us to seat six hundred people in a building that was semi-fireproof. The day after that law was passed these theatres were obsolete and we could not use them any more. Later we built theatres seating a thousand or fifteen hundred people. Roxy has made obsolete a lot of the theatres even larger than the thousand and fifteen hundred types.

Question: In your opinion, will the producer eventually control all the large exhibiting houses in the country?

Fox: I hope not. I hope that will be left for private individuals. The minute they start doing that, they go back to the old trust idea that I helped break up. I shall devote my life to prohibiting any man or group of men from forming a monopoly that would tend to prevent the motion picture from growing to its full height. It never will reach its full height until, in a nation like ours that has a population of 114,000,000, every man, woman, or child reads a newspaper, book, or magazine and, at least once a week, goes to a motion picture theatre.

Question: Are news pictures a popular branch of the business?

Fox: Yes; we call ours Fox News. For the first five years it lost approximately $3,000,000 and after that it turned to black ink. Whether it has paid back what we originally lost I do not know.

Question: How long was it before you went into the production field?

Fox: I started as an exhibitor and distributor of motion pictures and I was one of the licensees in this group of one hundred and twenty that I spoke of. They destroyed the hundred and nineteen and offered to destroy me. I did not begin to produce motion pictures until the Supreme Court of the United States said that was a vicious combine and must be dissolved. As soon as they dissolved, I entered into the making of motion pictures. That was about 1913. I think the dissolution order was some time in the latter part of 1912 or the early part of 1913. That was the case of the People against the Motion Pictures Patents Company and General Film Company. Those who made up that combine were Lubin, of Philadelphia, Pathé, of Paris, Edison, of New York, Biograph, of New York, Spear and Anderson, of Chicago, Kleine, of Chicago, Millais, of Paris, and three others who have slipped my memory. There were ten all together.

Question: Where did you get your film to exhibit while you were fighting the trust?

Fox: The court enjoined them from withholding the proper supply of pictures to our theatres until the court could determine as to whether we were right or wrong. When that order ran out they were summoned to Washington and told that unless they immediately made an agreement with the government to continue to supply those pictures the attorney-general would cease letting them take any more testimony for the purpose of preparing their defense but would order them to trial immediately.

12

A MAN WHO HATED WILLIAM FOX

Dream after dream ensues
And still they dream that they shall succeed;
And still are disappointed.

—WILLIAM COWPER

IN San Angelo, Texas, there is a Roxy Bar and Cafe, in Seattle the Roxy Cleaners, in Los Angeles the Roxy Tuxedo Shop, in New Orleans the Roxy Radio and TV Service and in Miami the Roxy Auto Body Works. And so immortality, thanks to similar retail establishments in each of the continental states, has come to Samuel Lionel Rothapfel, even though his nickname no longer endures in marble, bronze and "decorations of indescribable beauty" at Seventh Avenue and 50th Street, New York, in the original Roxy Theatre, with its 6,214 seats.

With technological and economic inevitability, this "Cathedral of the Motion Picture," "an acre of seats in a garden of dreams," designed by architect Walter W. Ahlschlager to materialize Roxy's own dream specifications, was demolished in 1960 to make way, appropriately enough, for the efficient, no-nonsense, no-decorations stainless steel and glass office building of the American Management Association.

Born in Stillwater, Minnesota, July 9, 1882, Sam was

sixteen when his mother died not long after his patriarchal father, fed up with teen-age dreaming, had ordered him never again to darken the doors of their flat on the lower East Side of Manhattan.

After drifting as messenger boy, bootblack and doing other odd jobs, he enlisted in the Marines when he was eighteen, and in seven years, which included action in China during the Boxer rebellion, he was promoted to sergeant. All his life he loved the Marines, which had given him a purpose in life, and his drill-sergeant mentality has left its impress on whole platoons of movie ushers.

Back in civilian life again, his first quarter century ended with little formal education, he found work in a hash house, a livery stable, a shoe store and as a ball player in the Northeast Pennsylvania League, where a coach, gargling on Rothapfel, called him Roxy and unwittingly provided him with his tag for success.

One day in December, 1907, with baseball in cold storage, he was peddling books in Forest City and stopped for a beer and frankfurter in the bar operated by Julius Freedman, who was also the town undertaker. As he peered through the door into the large dance hall in the rear, he found Destiny waiting, for the proprietor's pretty daughter Rosa was tidying up after a coal-miners' party in the room that was to become the first Roxy Theatre.

This glib man of the world, who knew China and New York, soon talked himself into a job as a bartender and, with Rosa's help, persuaded her father that the back room, with a sheet hung at one end, and a projector at the other, could easily be transformed into a moving picture theatre. If some brothers named Warner could run a nickelodeon in New Castle, way out in western Pennsylvania, Forest City could certainly support its own nickel show.

As he hand-cranked his Lubin Marvel Cineograph, even the ambitious Roxy could never have dreamed that two decades later another Lubin (Herbert) would build a monumental movie palace just for him.

Although Sam never got farther than the sixth grade and knew nothing about music, he seems to have absorbed, in his travels, a sensitivity to cultural packaging, for his very first program at the Family Theatre, of three Vitagraph reels for five cents, also included a piano solo, a girl violinist and a baritone solo.

As word got around beyond the confines of Pennsylvania that the Family Theatre had class, the biggest theatre owner of them all, Benjamin Franklin Keith, sent for the owner and manager of the Family Theatre, and was so impressed by his enthusiastic showmanship that he hired him to make a tour of Keith Theatres and improve their motion picture presentations, for in those days films were regarded as chasers to get the audience out before the vaudeville acts came on again.

While traveling and studying theatres for Keith, Rothapfel met Herman Fehr, who was taking a licking with vaudeville at the Alhambra Theatre in Milwaukee. When Roxy prescribed photoplays that told a story, which were just then becoming available, Fehr hired him and authorized him to spend $5,000 to fix up the Alhambra for films. Fehr screamed that he was being bankrupted when Roxy went way over budget, but his magic worked so well that three months later the Saxe Brothers, who had other Wisconsin theatres, paid Fehr a $40,000 profit to get operating control.

Just a decade after his father had thrown him out, Sam decided that there must be theatres to doctor in New York, and he soon discovered that the new Regent, at Seventh Avenue and 116th Street, could not make out against the competition of B. F. Keith's Alhambra in the same neighborhood. The owner, who had tried everything, gave Roxy carte blanche, and he provided an atmospheric musical presentation for *The Last Days of Pompeii* that impressed even the great David Belasco.

The instant success of the ailing Regent established Roxy's success as a showman, and he was now able to march in triumph down to Broadway, on which he left his mark successively on the Strand at 47th Street, the Rialto at 42nd Street, the Rivoli at 49th Street and the Capitol across Broadway at 51st.

During the war years between 1914 and 1918, when Mary Pickford and Douglas Fairbanks were selling war bonds and everybody was hating the Huns, Rothapfel dropped the Germanic p in his name and became Rothafel, just as sauerkraut patriotically became Liberty Cabbage.

Built with DuPont and other war-boom money, the Capitol was by far the most luxurious theatre in New York. Thomas W. Lamb, the architect, lavished on its interior all the decorative arts that he could not deploy while designing the Strand, Rialto and Rivoli. But when it opened October 24, 1919, under the direction of Major Edward Bowes, the Capitol ran up such an operating deficit that even General Coleman T. DuPont cried for help, and sent for ex-sergeant Rothafel, who by now was an honorary major in the Marines.

Destiny, with new technology, again was waiting for Roxy in this dream palace, its cushioned seats hardly in the league with those undertaker's chairs back in Forest City. As engineers from the Bell Telephone Laboratories researched in the new theatre, trying to achieve remote control broadcasts, they finally got a microphone adjusted to their telephone lines, and there was Samuel Lionel Rothafel ready to step up and modulate it with music, comedy and homily, and before long radio station WEAF and its Blue Network had a lion by the tail.

From the moment of its triumphal reopening June 4, 1920, the Capitol was such a success that Major Bowes could only sulk in his luxurious apartment, with its private box looking down on the Roxy stage shows.

Those who came in late, and may never have heard of Roxy and His Gang on those folksy pre-TV Sunday nights, may find it difficult to believe that one man, with natural sentiment and contrived sincerity, so dominated the countryside that the people out there in Radioland could not go to sleep until the good uncle at the Capitol Theatre had given his benediction: "Good Night, Pleasant Dreams, God Bless You."

Theatre owners complained that Roxy was keeping millions from going to the movies but there was nothing they could do to deter this natural phenomenon as, from November 19, 1922, until July 26, 1925, Roxy ruled the airwaves.

Suddenly, on the last Sunday in July, 1925, Major Rothafel pulled his friendly enemy Major Bowes up to the microphone and, tears in his voice, choked up and sobbed, "Say goodbye to them for me. I can't." The ominous message: Major Bowes would carry on with the radio program but Roxy and His Gang would no longer be on the air, for the master of ceremonies was leaving the Capitol to supervise the building of his very own theatre.

"The Roxy—and I am prouder of the name than I am of my own—will be the fulfillment of my dreams of the last fifteen years. I will be the absolute despot of it. I have always wanted to present pictures as I think they should be presented, and with the opening of the Roxy Theatre I shall be hampered in no way whatsoever in having complete control over every detail, no matter how large or small."

If William Fox read that interview in the *New York Morning Telegraph* of December 20, 1925, he was too busy expanding his theatre chain to pay much attention. But three years later I was to discover that even the largest theatre in the world was not big enough to contain two absolute despots.

The old street car barns that used to occupy most of the block east of Seventh Avenue on 50th Street were still there, in 1925, abandoned for newfangled buses, when Herbert Lubin and Arthur H. Sawyer acquired an option to buy the land for three million dollars. By begging, borrowing and selling millions of dollars worth of stock to some thirteen thousand of Roxy's solvent listeners, they started excavation and construction of the monument to Roxy's most grandiose dreams. By Christmas, 1926, when the theatre was scheduled to open, the harassed promoters realized that neither Wall Street underwriters nor the people out there in Radioland had any commitment to provide pleasant dreams, up to ten million dollars, for their erstwhile Sunday night Godblesser.

When the Roxy opened March 11, 1927, the financial situation was so desperate that, ten days later, they sold control to William Fox, who for twelve million dollars acquired the enterprise. But if Fox was angel to Sawyer and Lubin, he was the very devil to Roxy.

"The Cathedral of the Motion Picture," with 6,214 seats monogrammed R, opened with an overwhelming presentation that postponed, smothered and confused *The*

Love of Sunya, which Gloria Swanson had personally produced for United Artists after rejecting a long-term contract for $20,000 a week from Adolph Zukor. In his excitement after watching Gambarelli and fifty ballet dancers and the precision Roxyettes and digesting a choral group of a hundred voices backed up by the largest symphony orchestra in existence and three organists highlighted on three consoles manipulating the largest theatre organ in the world, the projectionist squirted the final silent reel of Gloria's "greatest dramatic triumph" into the middle of the picture. By that time it was well past midnight and nobody much cared except the producer-star herself, the Marquise de la Falaise de la Coudraye, a one-time Mack Sennett cutie from Chicago.

The Roxy had been equipped with Vitaphone, which was the new Warner Brothers synchronization of a phonograph record with a film on which Al Jolson and others spoke their amplified words, but silent pictures were the screen entertainment at the Roxy until the Fox-Case sound-on-film system was perfected in 1929. Such talking features as *The Cock-Eyed World* and *Sunny Side Up* shot business up to new highs, and more people and more money flowed into the Roxy than to any other movie theatre in the world.

The jubilation of William Fox and his producer Winfield R. Sheehan was not shared by Samuel L. Rothafel, who realized that his symphonic background music and mood presentations were his personal contributions to silent pictures, and he resented the cans of film that came into his theatre complete with music, and singing, dancing and talking actors. Whenever a new sound picture was booked into the theatre by Fox, Roxy protested that it did not harmonize with the stage shows he was planning.

Finally neither Roxy nor Fox would speak to each other, in the flesh or on the telephone, and Fox used to delegate me to go over from Tenth Avenue and tell that so-and-so that such-and-such a picture would open. In his luxurious office I cleaned up the message for the president of the Roxy-Lubin-Sawyer Corporation and he replied in marine sergeant vituperation for the president of Fox Films and Fox Theatres. This feud came to a climax one day when Fox sent for me.

"Tell that bastard who calls himself a major that if he isn't out of his office within twenty-four hours I will send Major Zanft over to throw him out of the theatre."

John Zanft was general manager of Fox Theatres and husband of the chic couturier Hattie Carnegie, but no chic rubbed off onto him. In five years I never heard him complete a sentence without "sonofabitch" or "bastard," which I assume he thought were essential parts of speech. Major Rothafel had more field service in the marines, but Major Zanft was louder.

Delivering this message was the saddest and most embarrassing chore that I executed for either Fox or Sheehan, and I sensed Roxy's emotional turmoil as he paced his monogrammed rug, woven just for him, past the Arthurian mantelpiece with its mementos of esteem from those who loved him, as he realized that all the grandeur he had created was now to fall into the hands of such barbarians as Zanft and Fox.

Back when his dream palace was only architectural sketches I had introduced him at a luncheon when the Associated Motion Picture Advertisers acclaimed him an immortal of the movies, and I had been among those present on his glorious opening night when he exclaimed, "Take a look at this stupendous theatre. It's the Roxy and I'm Roxy. I'd rather be Roxy than John D. Rockefeller or Henry Ford."

To avoid a brawl and public humiliation I advised him to go quietly. I told him how sorry I was, then left him to clean out his desk and remove his personal belongings from his suite with its electric grand piano, objects of art, two bedrooms, kitchen, dining room, steam room, massage table and cedar closets for his eighty suits.

Henry Ford stuck to his Model A and declined to become involved with Fox when he appealed to him in 1930 for desperately needed millions, but John D. Rockefeller, Jr., took note of this neighbor just a block west of his Center then aborning. Before long his son Nelson, then only governor of Rockefeller Center, was up to his ears in show business with the Radio City Music Hall and the RKO-Roxy on Sixth Avenue, a theatre so luxurious that even the Rockefellers couldn't afford to own it longer than from 1932 to 1946, when it was demolished to make room for an office building.

With the backing of Radio-Keith-Orpheum, a company put together by Joseph P. Kennedy, Roxy helped design, just as vaudeville was dying, the enormous vaudeville house that is now the Radio City Music Hall as well as the 2,200-seat film theatre (also called the Roxy) until litigation changed its name to the Center.

Roxy's vaudeville program which opened the 6,200-seat Music Hall on Tuesday, December 27, 1932, ran on until 2:30 Wednesday morning, and was a disaster. He retired sick, bewildered and defeated as the Rockefellers replaced the master showman with W. G. Van Schmus who, by his own admission, had seen only two movies in half a century. But this trusted caretaker transformed the Music Hall, with top pictures and subroxy presentations, into

"The Showplace of the Nation." It still lines up ticket buyers around the block waiting to get in to see the Easter and Christmas shows.

Four years later, before Roxy could try his magic at revitalizing the bankrupt original Roxy, he died, and a nephew named Rothafel, and many others, tried to make it pay until the Cathedral was razed in 1960.

13

ECLIPSE OF THE SUN

*It behooves the minor critic, who hunts for blem-
ishes, to be a little distrustful of his own sagacity.*

—JUNIUS

IN all the thousands of films produced before 1926 the
actors moved, but the camera did not. It normally
remained fixed and steady. Of course the camera had
traveled and photographed scenes from trains as far back
as 1903 when the inspired Fire Chief of Kansas City,
George C. Hale, had hand-cranked a camera mounted on
a flat car to record all the exciting rail scenery rushing
past moving trains.

The thrill of these early movies, enlivened by bells,
whistles and the clicketyclick of wheels on rails, comes to
me vaguely from the days when I was a boy in Kansas
City, and Twelfth and Main was the entertainment center
of my universe. In 1903, Hale's Tours moved from Electric Park in Kansas City to become the novelty sensation
of the World's Fair in St. Louis; and travel movies, in
wide screen, sound and color, are still bringing geography
to our eyes and ears.

But it was German innovators in the great pre-Nazi
UFA studios that demonstrated the dramatic potentials of

the mobile camera. America awakened to these cinematic possibilities when Paramount, in 1926, imported *Variety,* in which director E. A. Dupont and cinematographer Carl Freund set the camera swinging from a trapeze to record circus thrills, so that the lens became the eye of the actor.

The ingenious Freund also traveled his camera in *The Last Laugh,* as F. W. Murnau directed Emil Jannings in a memorable picture that brought both the director and the star to Hollywood. After hundreds of popular but unpretentious pictures starring Theda Bara, June Caprice, Tom Mix and Madge Bellamy had issued from the old Fox studios at Sunset and Western, Fox was awarded the very first Photoplay award for Frank Borzage's sensitive direction of Janet Gaynor and Charles Farrell in *Seventh Heaven.* Winfield Sheehan, who had bought Austin Strong's stage play and paired these two young lovers, now set his sights on artistry and imported from Germany the Heidelberg University graduate and associate of Max Reinhardt who had been acclaimed for his direction of *The Last Laugh.* With all the resources of Hollywood, Sheehan encouraged Murnau to employ his UFA artistry and his mobile camera in directing *Sunrise,* which he did with such startling results that the *Film Daily* reviewer was impelled to comment that "this masterful technical achievement is the finest accomplishment in production not only for this year but for all the years."

But when *Sunrise* opened in New York, some of the newspaper reviewers, unaccustomed to looking to Fox for art, reacted as if it was just another picture. *Sunrise* was the first of more than two hundred Fox features for which I prepared international advertising campaigns, and as I culled the reviews for quotes I was puzzled that some of the critics with intellectual pretensions had not discovered, as the trade paper reviewer had, that Murnau's "camera effects are amazing for the mind as well as for the eye."

For the first time since I had signed a five-year contract with him as director of advertising and publicity, William Fox sent for me.

"Who is this sonofabitch Cohen?"

"John S. Cohen is the reviewer on the *Sun,* a young man up from Atlanta who considers himself artistic."

"Did you read his review of *Sunrise?*"

"I certainly did."

"I'll fix that bastard. From now on the *Sun* is to get only ten lines of advertising on any Fox picture."

"Yes, Mr. Fox."

"Until you get a memo signed by me personally authorizing more space, the *Sun* will never have more than ten lines."

He was furious and I played it cool, telling the advertising agency and my assistants that there was to be no slip-up in scheduling space for the *Sun.* When their man on amusements telephoned that the other papers had big ads quoting glowing reviews on *Sunrise* and asked when would the *Sun* get the copy, I said, "Never." When he came rushing over to Tenth Avenue to see me, I told him that I was playing around with the budget and not giving the same space to all papers, but I did not confide that the president of the company had made the decision. I had known Neil Kingsley a long time but felt no obligation to confide in him about internal corporate matters, and he decided that I just did not like John S. Cohen.

Deprived of Fox display advertising, the *Sun* dropped to the bottom in all compilations of amusement lineage and, as this weakness was noted by space buyers in other classifications, the evening paper, which had absorbed the brilliant *Morning Sun,* began losing more space, especially to the colorful pictorial *Daily News.*

Keith Speed, the *Sun* editor who had known Winnie Sheehan when he was a reporter for the *World,* appealed to Sheehan in his capacity of vice president and general manager, but Sheehan lost many an argument with William Fox, and this was one of them. Not until after his final blow-up with Fox, when he and Saul Rogers and other executives joined up with the bankers who forced Fox out of the companies he had founded, did the paper get any Fox display advertising, but by then the *Sun* was setting. Seats you don't sell and ads you don't run never pay off retroactively. During this difficult period, the management of the *Sun* stood loyally behind its critic, and it was quite by accident that I learned from my homosexual homeopath that John S. Cohen had gone nuts, literally.

Once when I had a runny nose I called on Dr. Edmund Devol at his Fifth Avenue office near St. Patrick's Cathedral. The good doctor had the most charming bedside manner I have ever encountered, and for a decade after I first met him in our Greenwich Village apartment when he prescribed for Buck Crouse before either of us was married, I could hardly wait to get sick so that he could hold my hand and take my pulse.

He had been in Woodrow Wilson's party on his triumphal tour of Europe after the peace conference, and was an occasional escort of the president's daughter Margaret who, years later, retired to India for contemplation with a guru. Most of his patients were from the theatre, the literary set or the social register. When Alexander Woollcott lay dying in the NBC studios after his final broadcast that Sunday night in 1943, it was Dr. Devol he asked for, and Woollcott died in his arms.

The doctor gave me a prescription for my cold, observed that I was run down from working too hard, and said I'd feel better with colonic irrigation. As I stretched out, face down, on his work bench, and he washed out the residue of prohibition drinking and irregular eating, he gossiped about his famous patients.

"Know who was on this bench just before you came in?"

"I have no idea."

"Fannie Hurst."

"Really," and I counted ten to withhold comment, mindful of the Hippocratic oath of medical ethics. The doctor enjoyed his practice, and his sophisticated patients did not, I assume, mind being talked about or picking up scuttlebutt. He reported that only last night he had been wakened after midnight and hurried over to mediate a lovers' quarrel between Mayor Jimmy Walker and his Betty Compton.

He said that he and the Lutheran bishop with whom he shared his life had recently been dinner guests of Mrs. Edgerton Parsons, vice president of the League of Nations Association, whose daughter Tony my brother Earl had married after a romance that developed on a round-the-world cruise. The doctor asked about Earl and I inquired about Tony, who was divorced and living in Pasadena.

As I relaxed, ingesting a quart of acidophilus buttermilk, the doctor demanded: "Why do you hate John S. Cohen?"

"I don't hate Cohen and wherever did you get that idea?"

"He says that you keep picking on him and that he's in serious trouble with his job on the *Sun*."

"Is he one of your patients?"

"Not only a patient, but a friend, and I'm trying to help straighten him out. I played bridge with him one night last week, and he told me that you are the cause of his emotional breakdown. He is in bad shape, and may have to be sent to a sanitarium."

I explained to Dr. Devol that I was too vain to hate anybody, because active hate, I believe, shows in the face and eyes. And with sixty people in my department getting out promotional material for one feature picture every week, I had not time even to think of Cohen, let alone hate him.

"When you see Cohen please tell him that it is William Fox, and not I, who is having his revenge. I don't believe in fighting newspapers, for they always have the last word."

Quinn Martin, reviewer for the *World,* a sensitive introvert, also thought I did not like him, and for the silly reason that he had never gone to college—as if that could be valid in a business where few major film company presidents ever went to college. The rare exceptions were John Otterson during his year at Paramount and Robert H. O'Brien, who in 1963 ascended to the MGM throne previously occupied by Marcus Loew, Nicholas Schenck and Joseph R. Vogel. After the *World* folded and Quinn went to work at the Fox studio this former reporter on the *Kansas City Star* and I had a chance to get acquainted, as next-door neighbors in Hollywood, and we resolved whatever misconceptions we may have had about each other.

When I met Cohen or Martin or other reviewers at premieres or cocktail parties my attitude, I thought, was correct and courteous, but never conniving. With Fox, because of the head start on talking pictures, buying more newspaper space by far than any other company, I did not ever want to use advertising as a club or bribe for favorable reviews. My school of journalism ethics, I admit, could be confusing in a show business jungle where reviews were bought and sold for money, dames, apartment leases and charge accounts at luxury shops.

We all have our troubles. William Fox spent a year in the penitentiary. John S. Cohen was confined in a mental institution. I went into an emotional tailspin for six months after my play *Knights of Song* played only fourteen performances on Broadway after such enthusiasm in Pasadena and St. Louis that Oscar Hammerstein, who needed a success during the dry spell between *Show Boat* and *Oklahoma!*, declined outside financing because he knew he had a hit. The best of all the reviews for this musical biography of Gilbert and Sullivan was by Richard Lockridge, published in the *Sun*.

Back in New York, I was promoting Joe Cook in the ice show at the Center Theatre when my old friend Neil Kingsley, still hustling ads for the doddering *Sun*, came in with the first edition and a cartoon of Joe as he looked a quarter of a century ago in his first Broadway musical, in a nostalgic feature which the *Sun* nurtured along with its popular antiques pages. I should have counted ten, for there was a hurt look in his face as I said, "Thank you, Neil, I always look in the *Sun* when I want to know what was going on twenty-five years ago." I am sure he reported back to his publisher that I was still picking on the *Sun* long after John S. Cohen was in his grave.

This was confirmed a month later when, at a luncheon of the Banshees, a newspaper social group, I happened to be seated next to Publisher Dewart, who, when he heard my name, did a restrained double take as he finally met, in the flesh, the nemesis of his departed film critic.

When the final eclipse of the *Sun* came on January 4, 1950, I mourned the passing of an old friend, just as I had in 1930 when the Pulitzers could not afford to own the *World* any more.

Even the *Sun*'s memorial existence as a pendant to the *World-Telegram*'s masthead passed out in the 1967 folding of its merger with the *Journal-American* and the *Herald Tribune*.

At the turn of the century there were sixteen New York newspapers of general circulation. In 1967 there were three: the *Times,* the *News* and the *Post.*

In those days there was only one printer's union, and now there are nine additional newspaper unions, escalating wages with every contract of employment. Crushed between increased labor costs and declining advertising, not even a fortune like John Hay Whitney's could support the nine-million-dollar annual deficit of the corporate troika known as the *World Journal Tribune.*

In 1963 radio and television advertising in the New York metropolitan area totaled $76,462,433, which is revenue that used to keep newspapers alive, and which made the *Morning Sun* and the *Evening Sun* important media of communication before airwaves, curved for video and straight for radio, brought us instant electronic news.

14

THE FOX SWALLOWS THE LION

*Where the lion's skin will not reach, you must
patch it out with the fox's.*

—PLUTARCH

IN the pecking order of southern California the company
with more stars than there are in heaven looked down
from Culver City at Hollywood, Westwood, Burbank and
Universal City. If all the tycoon egos had been penned in
behind chicken wire, the head clucker would have inevitably put the lesser fowls in their descending order,
and Louie B. Mayer would have ruled the roost.

He always did, except during the transition months
from President Coolidge to President Hoover, when a
sneaky deal between President William Fox and President
Nicholas M. Schenck changed the peck order.

Imagine his humiliation and consternation when the
Sunset Limited pulled in to New Orleans Monday, March
4, 1929, and Mayer, vice president of Metro-Goldwyn-
Mayer, discovered from the newspapers that he was an
employee of William Fox, who had acquired control of
Loew's, Inc., and its subsidiary MGM by buying, above
market prices, the shares held by Schenck, David Bernstein, the Shuberts and the Loew family.

In his personal diversification from improving the breed of horseflesh, Mayer, the star maker, had tried his hand in grooming a secretary of commerce for the White House and had miraculously come up with a Potomac winner with the help of William Randolph Hearst and Mabel Willebrand, whom he had hired away from the United States Treasury Department.

To celebrate his colossal victory, Mayer was traveling with his wife and daughters, Mrs. David O. Selznick and Mrs. William Goetz, to be the first overnight guests of the new White House tenants, Mr. and Mrs. Herbert Clark Hoover. And now in his hour of triumph this contretemps, this denouement, this *et tu Brute!* No wonder Mayer couldn't sleep as he tossed in his White House bed which, inevitably, must have been that of Abraham Lincoln, another martyr.

While the Mayer party was crossing the Arizona desert, I was summoned to the Hotel Ambassador on Park Avenue to meet William Fox, and when Nicholas Schenck arrived with David Bernstein, treasurer of Loew's, Inc., I wondered what was going on. Sheehan told me that I was present at a really big deal, that Fox was buying Loew's.

Fox and Sheehan produced wallets and pulled out checks, which they handed to a Loew lawyer who was checking the contract of sale with Alvin Untermyer, son of the ailing Samuel. But the checks did not add up; there was a twenty-million-dollar shortage. Bernstein looked at Schenck as if to say I told you they were bluffing; Sheehan and Fox looked at each other, baffled. They searched their wallets, they checked the pockets of their jackets, they turned their trouser pockets inside out. Then in the small watch pocket of his trousers, Fox found the folded, crumpled certified check for twenty million dollars, and the deal was closed.

Now two diamonds in the rough had what they wanted. Schenck had a profit of around twenty million dollars. He had bought stock from Lee and Jake Shubert and David Warfield so secretively that not even J. Robert Rubin, Mayer partner and vice president and general counsel, suspected what was going on.

Now Fox could proceed with his plan of eliminating two hundred duplicate offices at home and abroad for a seventeen-million-dollar annual saving in distribution costs. He could also control the flow of the output of three studios into the hundred-odd Loew theatres and into his thousand theatres at home and abroad. Even if Paramount and Warner Bros. should get together in a merger then being discussed, Zukor and the three Warners would only have minority control, while Fox had Leo the Lion by the tail (Ars Gratia Artis) in his firm 53 per cent grip.

More stars than there are in heaven, and Irving Thalberg, too! When Schenck and Bernstein and the lawyers left, I shook the hand that ruled the motion picture industry.

I sent telegrams to all newspapers, press associations and trade papers announcing an important press conference at 4:00 p. m. Sunday, March 3, 1929, and everybody responded. My mimeographed release reported 400,000 Loew shares had been sold for $50,000,000. The Messrs. Fox, Sheehan, Schenck and Bernstein were there to confirm the deal and answer questions.

The news exploded like an intercontinental bomb in London and Los Angeles, but its major detonation was in New Orleans, when Mayer read the incredible announcement that it was now Fox-Goldwyn-Mayer.

On the long ride up from Dixie there was plenty of time to think about Mr. Skunk, as he then habitually referred to the man who had betrayed him. But before the angry confrontation in New York there was Tuesday, the glorious inauguration day when all of Washington acclaimed the great engineer and humanitarian as he became the thirty-first president of the United States. With Mayer money and strategy since that lucky day when he had jumped the gun on California and national Republicans and nominated the secretary of commerce for the presidency, Mayer now had a long-shot winner that would pay off. There are times when you can't top the Master Dramatist for dramatic situations.

Meantime Fox was shoring up his victory by secretive market buying, during March, April and May, through A. C. Blumenthal and others, of 260,900 shares of Loew stock, for a total of around $70,000,000. Much of this money was borrowed from Harry Stuart, who advised Fox: "For goodness sake own the majority, or you will be wiped out. You can see your danger."

"Several days later," Fox told Upton Sinclair, "the representative of the Telephone Company (presumably John E. Otterson, whom Fox then hated to the point of anonymity) called and said, 'You are in a fine spot, aren't you? You had better hurry and buy these shares before someone else does.'"

Was it a trap? Was the octopus sucking in his victim?

In scrambled zoology Sinclair agreed with his confessor: "I do not know whether foxes ever run in packs, but I have read about wolves, and have learned that a wolf is not attacked so long as he is well and strong, and is running at the head of the pack. It is only when something happens to him, so that he stumbles and falls, that the other wolves fall upon him and 'merge' him."

In March, 1929, Mayer's profitable percentage-of-the-profits deal with Loew's still had two years to go, and when he and Thalberg confronted Schenck and threatened to take their production talents away from Culver City, the fate of the company was in jeopardy. Under the terms of their contract, which provided that after the payment of dividends of two dollars per share of common stock, Mayer, Thalberg and Rubin were to split a 20 per cent bonus, they had been picking up, in addition to their salaries, three million dollars annually, more or less. A truce was patched up with Thalberg by cutting him in on $250,000 of the Schenck gravy, but Mayer was not appeased.

Before beginning their Loew acquisitions, Fox and Sheehan had taken the precaution to check with "Wild Bill" Donovan, attorney general for Calvin Coolidge, who told them in Arizona that he had no objection to the merger. But with the change in Administrations came a change in the Department of Justice. Fox called on Hoover, and during luncheon in the White House, told the president of his campaign contributions and of the enormous national influence of Fox Movietone News. The president was sympathetic and suggested that he send his general counsel to confer with the attorney general. After several futile conferences Saul E. Rogers reported that he was getting the runaround.

Soon Fox had a call from Colonel Claudius F. Huston of the Republican National Committee, who asked him if he knew Louis B. Mayer. Fox got the message, and offered Mayer a two-million-dollar bonus and a new percentage contract. But by then Mayer's position in the Administration was so strong that he aspired to be ambassador to Turkey, and he told Fox: "You must have known that I have moved heaven and earth to prevent this consolidation. Surely you felt that someone used his influence to have the government change its opinion with reference to these shares. I was responsible."

As a result, on November 27, 1929, just after the stock market crash, a suit was filed by the United States attorney general against Fox Film Corporation and Warner Brothers Pictures for restraint of trade. With their vast Vitaphone profits, Warner Brothers had acquired control of First National, an exhibitor group making and distributing pictures, from Fox, after Fox had picked up these shares incidentally when he bought control of Wesco. And now Justice, whether blind, righteous in the public interest, or politically motivated, lowered the boom on these wheeler-dealers.

On July 10, 1931, Judge John C. Knox, in the United States District Court, ordered Fox Film Corporation to divest itself of the Loew stock and assigned 660,900 shares to be voted by the Film Securities Corporation. Three trustees were appointed to guard the stock, the chairman being Winthrop W. Aldrich, president of the Chase National Bank and brother of Mrs. John D. Rockefeller, Jr.

With these legal safeguards, nobody at Fox dared confer with anybody at Metro-Goldwyn-Mayer. The mild-mannered Irving Thalberg, who had only been partly pacified by his bonus payment from Mr. Skunk, threatened to walk out of the Culver City studio if Winnie Sheehan ever entered.

Rampant over all, with the peck order now reestablished, Louis B. Mayer and his roaring lion gloated over the vanquished Fox.

15

PRESIDENT CLARKE

Resolved to take Fate by the throat and shake a living out of her.

—LOUISA MAY ALCOTT

THE banking house of Halsey Stuart & Co. Inc., in a March 24, 1930, letter to stockholders of Fox Film Corporation and Fox Theatres Corporation, appealed to them to vote for their financing plan and to reject plans submitted by Bancamerica-Blair (favored by William Fox) and financing proposed by Lehman Brothers and Dillon, Read and Co.

Harry L. Stuart, one of the three trustees of the voting trust agreement signed by William Fox and repudiated by him December 22nd, assured Winfield R. Sheehan, vice president and general manager of Fox Films, that "their interest was solely that of a financial banker who had underwritten $48,000,000 of obligations of the companies, and that they owed a definite obligation to security holders who were scattered all over the United States."

John E. Otterson, the other trustee, "stated that the Telephone Company had no intention to, and would not, in any future time, wish to acquire any stock in any of the Fox companies, or any other motion picture company."

Repeated appeals for receivership of the Fox companies in February and March, 1930, were taken under advisement by U.S. District Court Judge Frank J. Coleman, who directed that stockholders should hold a meeting March 5th to decide if they preferred receivership to the proposed financial plans. By a vote of 914,000 to 33,085, they chose the Lehman Brothers plan.

But Harry L. Stuart was unwilling to accept this decision, and his lawyers forced Judge Coleman to withdraw on a certificate of disqualification, whereupon Federal Judge John C. Knox was assigned to study the litigation. Still fighting for control of his companies, William Fox engaged successively the most distinguished and expensive of Wall Street lawyers: Colonel Joseph M. Hartfield, Charles Evans Hughes (former governor of New York, former secretary of state and future chief justice of the United States Supreme Court) and Samuel Untermyer, who was more to the Fox taste and better casting for the part.

Although ailing that winter and conserving his health by resting weekends at Atlantic City, Untermyer, at seventy-two, was still breathing fire after battling the bankers in the Pujo money trust investigation before the House committee on banking and currency back in 1912.

Fox discharged Colonel Hartfield when he seemed to be siding with counsel for J. P. Morgan and the Chase Bank and fired the former governor when he discovered that Charles Evans Hughes, Jr., as solicitor general of the United States, had ordered Fox to divest himself of the 660,900 Loew shares which Fox had asked father Hughes to conserve for his companies. Hughes had never before dealt with such an ornery client, and he retired for rest and contemplation to Bermuda, where he was tapped for the Supreme Court. He was too much of a gentleman to deal with the likes of William Fox.

Untermyer elected to fight his case in the newspapers. He used to summon me at least twice a week to his suite at the Hotel Ambassador (now the site of an office building at 299 Park Avenue) where, as he rested in bed, he dictated denunciations of the Telephone Company, which I passed along to the *Wall Street Journal* and the *Times* and the press associations.

His strident demands that the Telephone Company get out of the sound equipment business unnerved the Ivy League lawyers for J. P. Morgan and all the banks involved with AT&T and its subsidiaries Western Electric and Electrical Research Products. It was Fox against the wolves of Wall Street and the kind of fight that Untermyer enjoyed.

After months of battering away at his targets, Untermyer finally worked out a deal whereby a Chicago group, put together by Halsey, Stuart, would acquire the Fox voting shares from the Otterson-Stuart-Fox voting trust. In this settlement William Fox was paid two million dollars, Samuel Untermyer collected one million dollars, and arrangements were made satisfactory to the Chase National Bank for the transfer of control to Harley Clarke.

And where was all this money coming from, now that Samuel Insull, long-time Clarke associate in utility promotions, was having his own financial problems?

The money would materialize from the sale, for $48.50 a share, of 433,000 shares of voting trust certificates for common stock (no par value) of General Theatres Equipment, Inc., Harley Clarke's holding company for various odds and ends, including the 50 per cent interest he held with William Fox in Grandeur, Inc. Although

Clarke's prospectus of May 1, 1930, listed holdings of 90 per cent of the shares of National Theatre Supply and almost all the outstanding stocks of International Projector Corporation, William Fox insisted that GTE was "just a bag of wind." Two years later, when GTE went into receivership, the wind contact appeared to be 98.7 for stocks and 96.3 for bonds.

With 20-20 hindsight, probably neither the Chase Bank nor Harry Leonard Stuart nor Harley Lyman Clarke would have become involved with the Fox enterprises, but in 1930 they got what they wanted, and here is what they got.

The Chase National Bank of the City of New York got the voting trust certificates, Harley L. Clarke, W. F. Ingold and W. S. Hammons became voting trustees and the Corporation Trust Company of Chicago became the depository of 50,101 shares of Class B common stock (voting control) of Fox Film Corporation and not less than a million shares of Class A common stock, and of all the outstanding shares of Fox Theatres Corporation.

The chairman of the Corporation Securities Company was Samuel Insull, partner-promoter with Harley Clarke in various stock-watering ventures.

Elected president of Fox Films and Fox Theatres, Harley Clarke set out to clean up the mess he had so ardently coveted and to remake the companies so that he and his friends, and not William Fox and his relatives, could lap up the gravy. He certainly brought a fresh point of view to the business of which he knew so little, except as manufacturer and seller of equipment. To a knowledgeable show business insider it looked as if the tail were wagging the dog.

His new broom swept clean, especially in the 1,100

owned and controlled theatres, hundreds of which were remodeled and redecorated whether or not they needed extensive refurbishing. The thirty-one branch offices of Clarke's 90-per-cent-owned National Theatre Supply Corporation handled all of the business.

Harold B. Franklin, president of Wesco and an experienced operator of 550 Fox theatres west of Kansas City and Milwaukee, who held a contract by which he received 10 per cent of any increase in profits that he might produce, protested to Clarke that if from four to five million dollars were spent on renovations, it would cancel any profit that Franklin might make. For this insubordination, President Clarke settled President Franklin's contract, at a cost to Fox Films of about half a million dollars.

Clarke had his own lawyers, who did not like some of the five-year employee contracts any better than Clarke liked Franklin's, and they envied the general counsel who knew of every legal move since incorporation in 1915. One morning in April, 1930, when Saul E. Rogers arrived on Tenth Avenue, he found his office padlocked. He retired to his Fifth Avenue law office to await developments, and it was not long before more litigation erupted from this Pandora's box.

Despite the closing of the Harriman National Bank in New York and other banks from coast to coast, film business for Fox rolled on with the momentum of sound-on-film pictures, and Fox Movietone News was heard by a hundred million people every week, in nineteen languages, as it played in more theatres than the combination of all four competing newsreels, Pathé, Universal, MGM and Paramount.

One week at the Roxy, 186,000 people bought admissions to see Janet Gaynor and Charles Farrell in *Delicious,* establishing the 1930 record with $132,000. But the theatre's all-time high had come a year earlier, with $164,667 for *The Cock-Eyed World*, for which my department mounted a massive promotional campaign. Once, when business at the Roxy fell below $100,000 a week, we held an emergency meeting to probe what was wrong in the house that later, after the nearby Music Hall opened, was happy to gross $35,000.

From the only studios designed and built for sound pictures, Winfield Sheehan turned out such products as Will Rogers in *A Connecticut Yankee in King Arthur's Court*, Ann Harding in *East Lynne*, the adorable Shirley Temple in a series of pictures that won exhibitor acclaim and Janet Gaynor and Charles Farrell in pictures that won Photoplay and Academy awards.

In the United States and Canada, Jimmy Grainger sold the pictures and Clayton Sheehan traveled overseas to speed up distribution from the offices that his brother had established.

The vast international machine that William Fox built churned along on its own momentum, but Clarke sought to improve its image and issued, through a financial advertising agency, a position paper bound in gold, with assurances that "sound banking principles and business methods are adhered to . . . Fox securities merit the attention of conservative investors."

In this April, 1931, report Clarke noted that his corporation "now distributes its output throughout the world through its own exchanges and wholly-owned subsidiary corporations. There are 31 of these exchanges in the United States and Canada in daily touch with every theatre on the continent. . . . The corporation operates 100 of its own exchanges abroad serving every civilized country in the world except Russia and some whose civilization would be questioned by sociologists.

"The potentialities of this foreign business are indicated by the fact that Fox export sales last year increased approximately 55 per cent. This was owing in part to the growth of sound exhibition abroad. At the beginning of last year there were 1,941 theatres outside the United States and Canada wired for sound. By the end of the year 8,882 of the 38,534 theatres abroad had been wired for sound.

"Through subsidiaries the Corporation owns Hoyt's theatres operating 100 houses in Australia and has a controlling interest in Gaumont-British Pictures Corporation. This is the largest theatre group in Great Britain and operates more than 300 theatres."

In July, 1931, the use of the text "William Fox presents" was discontinued on main titles, and I received word, as director of advertising and publicity, to eliminate William Fox in all copy.

People whom Clarke could trust, usually associates from Chicago, were added to the payroll, and they all found the heady show business atmosphere more exciting than utilities. As they glowed with new-found power and light, one of them, possibly under the influence of the affirmative thinking of Mary Baker Glover Patterson Eddy, to which Clarke subscribed, came up with "Mr. Courage and Mr. Fear," two characters whose movietoned dialogue was designed to help disperse the increasingly depressive attitudes of the final Hoover years.

Clarke's enthusiasm for this constructive suggestion was such that he personally selected the actors and supervised the making of a series of short-shorts projected into a majority of United States theatres by Fox Movietone

News. In retrospect I surmise that psychologically Clarke himself was both Mr. Courage and Mr. Fear, as his super-ego debated with his id.

In the real life drama beyond his control, economic forces were shaping that sent his super-promoter crony Samuel Insull fleeing to Europe to escape the wrath of people who had been duped into buying Utilities Power and Light and other paper issued by the Insull-Stuart-Clarke enterprises.

When I was a freshman at the University of Kansas I studied Moulton's *Introduction to Astronomy,* and was surprised and pleased, fifteen years later, to have Clarke introduce me to his old friend and confidential adviser, Dr. F. W. Moulton, professor of astronomy at the University of Chicago. Now Clarke asked me to work with Dr. Moulton in preparing a brochure showing Fox Film Corporation in its most favorable light as a wholly owned subsidiary of General Theatres Equipment, with its head office at 624 South Michigan Avenue, Chicago.

Dr. Moulton had been in on the founding of this equipment company and he and Clarke, as fathers of small children a decade previously, had been drawn together by the home movies that each was making. Dr. Moulton thought he could improve on the 16-millimeter projectors then available and Clarke helped him finance a projector of his own design. After losing half a million dollars on this venture, Clarke decided to buy International Projector Corporation, which became a part of GTE.

All of the additional Clarke equipment companies, all outstanding shares of Fox Theatres and the priceless William Fox voting shares of Fox Film Corporation, were in 1930 controlled by three shares of one-dollar stock, one share held by Clarke, one share by W. F. Ingold (of

Pynchon & Company) and one share by W. S. Hammons of Hammons & Company. In 1931 these two principal underwriters of GTE stock went into bankruptcy, dragging down with them the venerable investment house of West & Company, established one year before the signing of the Declaration of Independence.

In June, 1932, the New York Stock Exchange delisted GTE, and in December the stock was removed from the New York curb market.

Total losses to GTE underwriters and stock buyers were around $225,000,000.

With unerring instinct Harley Clarke had known that an astronomer was needed to explain his blue sky.

16

FOX CHASE

A fox went out in a hungry plight
And he begged of the moon to give him light,
For he'd many miles to go that night
Before he could reach his den-O.

—THE GRAY GOOSE

O N Fifth Street in Philadelphia there used to be a
street car marked Fox Chase. It did not pass the huge
Fox Theatre, built in part with Chase Bank money and
the rest from the local financier Greenfield, as it headed
out into rural Pennsylvania.

These two words *Fox Chase* tell a melodramatic story
of how William Fox was chased by a pack of avaricious
bankers until he dropped exhausted, bankrupt and almost
dead, and how a Harrisburg judge lodged him in a Pennsylvania prison.

When the Chase Bank finally realized what Harley
Clarke was doing to the Fox companies, they invited him
to go back to Chicago with his cronies Insull and Stuart.
Then they rushed to the rescue Edward Richmond
Tinker, president of the Chase Securities Company and
board chairman of the Chase National Bank. Tinker was
a banker's banker, more expert in evaluating consolidated
balance sheets than appraising the potential net worth of
Shirley Temple.

If Tinker and Wiggin and other Chasemen loathed the

contemptible William Fox, who hated back, doubled in clubs, they at least knew that being kicked in their groins was just standard Fox gutter-style infighting.

But Harley? He was couth and smiling and ingratiating and a gentleman, the luncheon and nighttime playboy companion of the Boston Brahmin, Albert H. Wiggin, the Chase Bank president who testified before the Senate investigating committee that he had lost $1,572,753 in his manipulation of Clarke's General Theatres Equipment stock.

What Clarke did to the Chase Bank hurt more than anything Fox said or tried to do, for he was one of their own trusted advisors. And it was Clarke's own boy scout Donald E. McIntyre whose naïveté in Sheehan's wire-tapped studio had boomeranged so that only the power of big money had kept some Chase bankers from being arrested for criminal libel against Sheehan.

When interviewed after his election as Fox Film president November 7, 1931, Tinker was disarmingly frank, and admitted that he did not know anything about running a motion picture company. He said that he would try to recruit a new staff of executives.

After nineteen months of Clarke operations, he had his work cut out for him. Never before, as a banker in Wall Street and on Park Avenue and at his Woodbury farms at Syosset on Long Island, had he encountered such fantastic people and such insoluble problems. Compared to a twenty-million-dollar profit in the last year of William Fox he discovered that in 1931 the company had a net loss, after taxes, of $4,263,557.

Obviously the operating costs had to be slashed out in the Westwood factory where his investigator McIntyre was reporting incredible salary contracts with actors, writers, directors and producers. With the prestige of the

Rockefeller bank behind him, now that Wiggin had been eliminated, why not just cancel these contracts, beginning at the top with Sheehan's $400,000-a-year contract which next year would escalate to a cool half million?

These were contracts that his friend Clarke had made, with the approval of the Chase-dominated board of directors—such financiers as Matthew C. Brush, Samuel W. Fordyce, David K. E. Bruce and Cornelius Vanderbilt.

When Tinker and McIntyre walked into Sheehan's Movietone City, which he had so lovingly built in 1928 for sound recording, they discovered that Sheehan knew more about sound—and the sound of their quibbling complaints—than all their formidable financiers and lawyers.

But the pressure on Sheehan, always a volatile tycoon accustomed to having his way—sometimes even with William Fox—built up so that on January 20, 1932, on the verge of a nervous breakdown, Sheehan was given a three-month leave of absence. President Tinker was careful to explain, with harrowing memories of how Sheehan's lawyer Nathan Burkan had enforced his contract on a previous leave, that Sheehan was not out, just out of the running because of exhaustion. His long-time assistant, Sol Wurtzel, would carry on with production, assisted by Al Rockett, who had previously made pictures for First National and Paramount.

Meantime, over at Paramount, which was on the verge of bankruptcy, with a thousand theatres running up weekly losses, Sidney R. Kent had resigned as vice president, after fourteen years as Zukor's dependable right-hand man and super-salesman. He, too, was exhausted from his battles with Sam Katz and B. P. Schulberg and Jesse L. Lasky.

After a long rest in Florida he took an office in Wall Street and there this former coal miner made himself available to diagnose ailing film companies, which included just about all of them except Warner Brothers and Metro-Goldwyn-Mayer. He had discussions with Joseph P. Kennedy about Radio-Keith-Orpheum, then in receivership, and with the Chase Bank about its loans and the stocks of its Chase Securities Company.

In receivership also were the Skouras theatres in St. Louis, the Poli chain in New England, the Fox Metropolitan circuit in New York. Many Paramount affiliates, and theatres from coast to coast, were in trouble as people stayed away from box offices by the millions. Because there were few blockbuster attractions? Because the novelty of sound had waned? Because of the national depression? Who, in Wall Street or Hollywood, was smart enough to know the right answers?

"There is nothing in this business which good pictures cannot cure," observed Nicholas M. Schenck, president of Loew's and Metro-Goldwyn-Mayer.

Did Wurtzel and Rockett, with Sheehan recuperating, have the shrewd mastery of turning out great moneymakers without the established stars that the banker could not afford? The stars on which Schenck and Mayer seemed to have a monopoly?

Who could tell? Certainly not Tinker, or his adviser Kent, or even Cornelius Vanderbilt or his namesake and relative, Cornelius Vanderbilt Whitney, who later made shrewd investments in Technicolor and *Gone with the Wind,* along with his cousin John Hay Whitney.

But the banker-president was philosophical about his corporate woes:

"The film industry," he announced, "is at that final stage of development which all young industries reach when their principal units become public companies and cease to be the private concern of pioneers."

17

MORE MALICE

Where the grapes of wrath are stored.

—JULIA WARD HOWE

POOR hounded Fox! In 1932 and 1933 there was no place to hide. Not on the confessional couch of social scientist Upton Sinclair or beneath Rubens's "Madonna and Child with Saints" at Fox Hall. The pack was after him in full cry. He could play sick and be sick, but they flushed him out.

In Washington, where he had been summoned by Senate subpoena, he was bedded down with a severe cold, but neither doctors' certificates nor lawyers' pleadings could protect him.

"I prohibit you from going anywhere where you will have a mental disturbance," decreed the Washington physician who had been summoned and who diagnosed biliousness, pains in gall bladder and appendix, and diabetes. Two doctors sent by the Senate Investigating Committee to check on malingering confirmed that the reluctant witness was not merely indisposed to appear.

Not that he had not asked for this public forum. With Fox approval, Upton Sinclair had wired Senator James

Couzens of Michigan, Republican defender of high finance, to suggest looking into the stock manipulations of Percy Rockefeller and Matthew C. Brush, a 1931 director of Fox Film Corporation, hoping that Senate evidence would reveal that Harry Stuart, Harley Clarke and Albert H. Wiggin had been selling short. Inadvertently Fox had walked right into this trap.

William A. Gray, a Philadelphia criminal lawyer who was counsel for the Senate Banking Committee, had been denouncing Fox as a wrecker, and he demanded that Fox get out of bed and talk. Gray's headlines were going great but they would be bigger with an in-the-flesh heavy— with a big, bad Fox. Back in Iowa, in Idaho, in Nebraska, let the constituents know that they had elected to high office men of righteous indignation who were in the nation's capital to protect them from malefactors of great wealth. Flush out the Fox.

He came, a diabetic with runny nose, rheumy eyes and aching head to face his tormentors, without legal counsel.

"That is a fine trap to be caught in; a fine trick for the United States Government to lend itself to. The octopus, of course, knew all about this," observed the indignant Upton Sinclair.

Testifying June 8, 1932, Fox admitted being in a stock pool conducted by manager Ellsworth, along with Walter Chrysler, John S. Raskob and Matthew F. Brady, which cleared $1,957,000 for the group. Gray expressed his annoyance when Fox was vague about some thirty brokerage accounts of his own and relatives, and the witness tried to explain: "I was deprived of my records, the company was captured and I had no control and have no control of the records now."

Q. Personal records?

A. Everything I had is in their hands.

Q. Whose hands?

A. In the hands of my enemies.

Q. Who got your personal records?

A. My personal files are intermingled with the company files, and they are lying there now, and we must beg or plead to go through the files for an individual letter. If you had known all that I had gone through from the day that I met with that accident until I sold out, you will recognize that I have no way of answering many questions you asked. I have no way and it is humanly impossible.

According to the Associated Press of June 17th, "Mr. Fox had freely admitted to him, Mr. Gray said, that he had manipulated Fox stocks to maintain a public market; that he believed short selling a rotten practice, but that he would continue it as long as the New York Stock Exchange permitted it, and that he would do it again."

After studying millions of words of testimony printed in documents issued by the Senate Finance Committee, Congress enacted laws during the first years of FDR's Administration with the help of Joseph P. Kennedy, first chairman of the Securities and Exchange Commission, that retarded but have not eliminated short selling.

More positively, thanks to legislation signed by President Roosevelt, security affiliates have been outlawed and banks can no longer gamble with depositors' money.

William Fox had strong convictions about these bank affiliates: "This, in my opinion, is nothing more than a gambling scheme to use funds belonging to depositors for speculation.

"A bank's function is carefully limited by the charter granted from either the State or the Federal Government;

whereas the function of a securities company is limited only to what the directors of the bank wish to incorporate in their certificate of incorporation. Usually that is so broad that it permits a securities company to do anything, and surely all the things that were never intended when the charter to the bank was granted. One need go no further than to read the charter of the Chase Bank, which was issued seventy-five years ago, to see what the wise fathers intended the bank to do; and then see what the Chase Securities Company can do now. But I don't intend this criticism for the Chase people only; a majority of the banks of the United States now have an affiliate; this is true of both large and small banks. The honest banker of thirty years ago has become a stock manipulator, using the funds of his bank to participate in various syndicates that are offered to him.

"Attached to the certificate of stock of the Chase Bank today are your rights in the Chase Securities Company. The stockholder knows definitely that his bank is not only a bank, but it has a securities company, and a securities company has unrestricted powers. If that were not so, Wiggin could not have been a planner with Clarke to capture my companies, nor could he make personal gains in his personal relationships with Clarke.

"Do you suppose Clarke wants Wiggin with him just because he is Wiggin? Or is it because he is the chairman of the board of the Chase Bank, and can manipulate $350,000,000 belonging to stockholders and $1,650,000,000 belonging to his depositors? I don't believe Clarke would be willing to be associated with the head of the Chase Bank or the head of any other bank who had only the privileges granted to him by the charter of the state or federal government.

"Of course the National City Bank also has a large securities company and many affiliates. The thing that destroyed the Bank of the United States was its affiliates. This is the most damnable practice that the banking world of this country has ever known; and the most necessary legislation I know of, by this Congress or any other Congress since the history of our government, is a law compelling the dissolution of these affiliates and securities companies. The surest way to make a banker be a banker and have the respect of the community he had before this began is to stop him from becoming a speculator.

"It was never intended that a banker should be a competitor of industry. A depositor or a borrower in a bank always felt free to go to the president of his bank and tell him of his tribulations, of his prosperity. You don't dare to do that now or they will take your company away from you."

The Fox at bay at long last flushed out his tormentors, and the next day Winthrop W. Aldrich, president of the Chase National Bank, produced records for the Senate investigators which revealed that his bank had gambled recklessly with depositors' money on film and equipment stocks, resulting in a total loss written off in the latest annual report as $69,572,180.44.

18

A DECADE OF KENT

*The romantic hero is no longer the knight, the cow-
puncher, the brave young district attorney, but the
great sales manager . . . whose title of nobility was
"go-getter" and who devoted himself and his young
samurai to the cosmic purpose of selling.*

—SINCLAIR LEWIS IN *Babbitt*

IT was angle and reverse angle in the transition from a
banker president who admitted he knew nothing about
film business to a distributor who knew every detail of
block booking and percentage dealing. Up in the higher
echelons of the Chase National Bank somebody had made
an astute selection when he picked Sidney R. Kent as the
fourth president of Fox Film Corporation.

Kent was a handsome super-salesman born in Nebraska's
capital city of Lincoln, which was considered an eastern
center of culture and sophistication by most of the population of Wahoo, Nebraska, renowned as the birthplace
of Darryl F. Zanuck.

Kent's own tabloid autobiography, either dictated or
approved for publication in the Who's Who of film business, is reprinted in its entirety from the *International
Motion Picture Almanac,* edited by Terry Ramsaye for
Quigley Publications:

"b. Lincoln, Neb. and at 14, after he had finished grammar school, got his first job stoking boilers in a greenhouse

at $5 a week. From this humble beginning he has de-
veloped a business career which is one of the most strik-
ingly successful ones in the annals of the picture industry.
Before he was 20 years old he had pushed up in Wyoming
and was occupying a responsible position with Colorado
Fuel and Iron Company. He was one of an engineering
company and he and five other men were the sole in-
habitants of 36 miles of desolate country. They built
their own roads and pipelines, established camps and
literally opened up territory to civilization and business
activity.

"In 1912 he went to the Pacific Coast with the American Druggists' Syndicate. Shortly afterwards he returned
east where he became a salesman at $50 a week. Three
months later he was the company's assistant sales manager,
then assistant to the president and for three and one-half
years he was virtually in charge of the entire business.

"A friend talked to him enthusiastically of the motion
picture business. He liked its prospects and cast his lot
with the old Vitagraph Company. It was not long after
that General Film Company was indicted under the Sherman law and buried under judgements aggregating
$25,000,000. Frank Hitchcock had the job of unravelling
the tangle and he called Sidney Kent to help him.

"The job was cleaned up and he walked into the office
of Adolph Zukor, president of Famous Players, and sold
his services, but not at a price. That was to be determined
if and when he made good. He went to work in the company's administrative bureau, and at the end of eight
months was getting $250 a week. His first work, in the
distribution department, was as special district manager
of the territory which included the Kansas City, St. Louis,
Omaha and Des Moines offices, which position he held

until May, 1919, when he was called to the home office to become general sales manager.

"On January 8, 1921, Zukor appointed him general manager of distribution and a year later he was elected to the company's board of directors. In 1927 he was named general manager. Was also vice president.

"Resigned in January 1932 to become Fox president. Largely instrumental in merging Fox Film Corp. with Twentieth Century Pictures, Inc. in August 1935 into Twentieth Century-Fox Corp. of which he is president."

Largely instrumental, in retrospect, in molding the company into what it is today; for the changes Kent made established new patterns for production, distribution and exhibition.

Winfield Sheehan had created such a sound international system of distribution that the Famous Players-Lasky Corporation came in second, and, from the viewpoint of Adolph Zukor and Sidney Kent, that was not Paramount.

When Kent was elected president of Fox, he had a healthy respect for Sheehan, who had emerged from his quarrel with William Fox with a five-year contract as general manager and vice president in charge of production. Although Sheehan lived in a Mediterranean castle at 1197 Angelo Drive in Beverly Hills and Kent was domiciled on Park Avenue in New York, the distance between them was greater than 3,025 miles. In brief, Sidney did not love Winnie. When Kent took over in January, 1932, he inherited a 1931 deficit of $2,851,996.98.

The year 1933 was a disaster for the film business. Bad as it was for Fox, it was worse for RKO, which started on its road to production extinction; and for Paramount-Publix it was bankruptcy.

In February, theatre losses in the West Coast theatres

became unbearable, and the Wesco Corporation went bankrupt. The court appointed Charles Skouras as receiver, and he put his younger brothers Spyros and George to work cutting expenses.

In March, the Fox Midwest Theatres went into receivership, and theatre business was so bad that in Kansas City forty houses closed, many of them never to reopen.

In June, the 1932 loss for Fox Film and its subsidiary Wesco was announced as $16,964,498 by Edward R. Tinker, who then resigned as chairman of the board.

But on September 30th, Kent was able to announce a small operating profit for the first time since 1930. His employers at the bank showed their appreciation by giving Kent a new three-year contract, and Kent issued a three-year contract to his distribution man from Paramount, John Clark, making him general sales manager. That sent Sheehan's man Jimmy Grainger packing, and soon only a presidential R would remain out of Edward R. Tinker, James R. Grainger and Winfield R. Sheehan.

As if to dramatize the financial errors of Fox and Clarke, $29,600,000 of canceled Fox Film Corporation bonds were burned in the furnace of the Chemical Bank & Trust Company in October, 1933. Present at these crematory rites were Sidney Towell, treasurer, Felix Jenkins, general counsel, and the executive vice president and Chase Bank man, W. C. Michel.

Kent returned from a studio visit to announce in New York the return of prosperity due to better pictures, which was an old cliché he had often used at Paramount, but what else can a salesman say about the product of a fantastic factory that manufactures a new model every week?

Cavalcade, the Noel Coward bittersweet story of a

British family, had been given such a superlative production by Sheehan that it won the Academy and many other awards, but Sheehan was not a Kent man or even a Chase man after he had charged the bankers with criminal libel and made them retract their accusations against him.

But how could Kent break Sheehan's contract when Wall Street lawyers had failed? Perhaps by wounding his vanity and dignity and pride in the company he had helped create, and bringing in a man twenty years younger to replace him.

Consultation with Nicholas Schenck, president of Metro-Goldwyn-Mayer, revealed that brother Joe would be willing to let him have Darryl Zanuck as head of production if Kent would arrange a merger with their Twentieth Century Productions. Those were the terms, and Kent convinced his bankers that their vast international system of theatres and selling offices would wither without the continuing flow of big pictures that Zanuck could provide.

It was a lopsided merger, like Mickey Mouse swallowing Dumbo, for Twentieth Century Productions had only the residual value of about twenty pictures produced in two years, no studio, no theatres and no film exchanges at home or abroad, in contrast with the Fox Film worldwide empire worth more than two hundred million dollars. Indeed, practically its only assets weighed in at about 300 pounds on four feet.

But the fifty-five-year-old Schenck, packaged with his brother at Loew's, Inc., was even more powerful than Louis B. Mayer, and in the thirty-three-year-old Zanuck Kent had his Thalberg, or at least the future winner of the Irving Thalberg awards for outstanding productions in 1939, 1944 and 1950.

As Kent had anticipated, when Zanuck was merged into

production, the producer of *Sunny Side Up* and *The Cock-Eyed World* threw in his Movietone, and S&Z swallowed the Fox. Now nobody cared what Sheehan thought, and the erstwhile world dictator retired to his Hidden Valley ranch and brushed up on his German so that he could talk to his wife's Lippizaner horses, a magnificent troupe which had been presented by Austrian nobility to Jeritza before the Metropolitan opera star became Mrs. Sheehan.

Fresh thinking and an increased flow of color pictures using the CinemaScope squeeze lens stepped up product and profits, as Zanuck gave creative reins to Nunnally Johnson, Joseph L. Mankiewicz, Kenneth Macgowan and others who could function as writers, directors and associate producers.

Bigger and better flowed the pictures and the profits until in 1939 Zanuck produced net profits of $4,146,813, followed by a 1940 loss of $517,336 and a 1941 profit of $4,921,926.

The year 1942 brought two ominous developments. With World War II going badly for us, Zanuck relinquished his studio responsibilities, turning production over to Buddy Adler. Commissioned lieutenant colonel in the U.S. Signal Corps, he saw active service in North Africa, and in 1943 was awarded the Legion of Merit.

On March 14th Sidney R. Kent died, and a decade of Kent segued into two decades of Skouras.

19

BANKRUPTCY AND PRISON

What though the field be lost?
All is not lost—th' unconquerable Will,
And courage never to submit or yield.

—JOHN MILTON, *Paradise Lost*

WHEN the bankers refused to renew his loans in 1930 and their security companies and Wall Street underwriters concentrated on putting their own houses in order, the unconquerable Will Fox tried desperately to convert his declining assets into cash, but an avalanche of debts overwhelmed him. Day by day he fought to stave off disaster as judgments and court orders piled up on him.

In 1932 Fox Theatres Corporation was forced into equity receivership on petition of Chicago Title and Trust Company, claiming $410,000 on a note signed by William Fox. Fox Metropolitan Theatres, then operating 175 houses, also was put into bankruptcy, with receivers appointed by the larcenous Federal Judge Martin T. Manton, whose wholesale vending of judicial favors had not then been uncovered.

By June, 1936, there was no way out for Fox except voluntary bankruptcy, and the man who had estimated that he was worth about one hundred million dollars in 1930 filed in Atlantic City a schedule listing his assets as $100 and his personal liabilities as $9,935,261.

Six years later, two cents were paid to creditors for each dollar owed them. When some of the judicial skulduggery in Fox personal and corporate receiverships had been ventilated, one federal judge was in the penitentiary and another was free.

Snarling at the enemies that surrounded him, the trapped Fox used every instinct of cunning in his fight for survival. He had been privy to the buying and selling of judges in the Tammany jungle, and all around him was evidence of the power of money. In his desperation he could always find lawyers who would go along with judicial fixers, one of whom called on him in Atlantic City to report that the federal court judge who was handling his bankruptcy application needed money to provide his daughter with a suitable wedding. Testifying under oath before three special masters appointed by the U.S. District Court, Fox said that he paid this bagman $15,000 and that the judge had personally thanked him. Later, by appointment, he met the judge on a Philadelphia street and handed him a newspaper containing $12,500.

These payoffs were discovered, and evidence was presented charging conspiracy to make loans totaling $27,500 to Judge J. Warren Davis, presiding in these bankruptcy hearings in United States District Court.

Indictments were issued against Judge Davis and Morgan S. Kaufman of Scranton, Pennsylvania; after two jury trials these indictments were withdrawn. But identical evidence found Fox guilty of conspiracy to bribe the judge who, by legal determination, was never bribed.

A jury found Fox guilty of obstructing justice and of defrauding the United States in bankruptcy proceedings, and on January 17, 1941, Federal Judge Guy K. Bard fined him $3,000 and sentenced him to a year and a day in the penitentiary. He was taken in Moyamensing Prison November 16, 1942, and was later transferred to North-eastern Federal Prison at Lewisburg, Pennsylvania.

Two years earlier, in this same penitentiary, Judge Martin T. Manton had served nineteen months for con-spiracy to sell his judicial favors. During Manton's twenty-three years as senior judge of the United States Circuit Court of Appeals, his bagman, William J. Fallon, had arranged loans totaling $439,481 to the judge and his corporations. Evidence revealed that during his years on the bench Judge Manton had an income of more than a million dollars, of which only one fourth was his salary.

The long-term lease on the Academy of Music, on which William Fox had arranged a reduction with the Boston landlords two decades earlier, now was further reduced by Judge Manton after alleged receipt of $30,000 from George Skouras, operating this and other Fox theatres in receivership, according to an indictment issued against Skouras, charging conspiracy to bribe a judge to approve a settlement favorable to Skouras contrived by William C. Weisman, receiver for Fox Theatres Corpora-tion.

As he brooded in his prison cell, who shall say that William Fox had not earned the right to a jaundiced view of the majesty of the law?

20

THE COMEBACK TRAIL

What the hell! A movie is a dream, and anything can happen in a dream.

—GARSON KANIN

WEARING a rumpled prison suit, the tycoon of yachts, Rolls-Royces and private railroad cars, on the morning of May 3, 1943, passed through the heavy steel-barred gates he had known so well in his own filmed melodramas such as *Up the River.*

As Fox made his final exit from the Northeastern Federal Prison at Lewisburg, the warden personally handed him a five dollar bill to start him on his comeback trail.

There were kisses from his devoted wife Eve and from daughters Mona and Belle, who hustled him off to their chauffeured limousine. Breathing again the clean free mountain air of Pennsylvania and the sour incinerations of the New Jersey marshlands and the soot and carbon monoxide of downtown Brooklyn, they rode past the five-thousand-seat Fox Theatre, its marquee alive with Bela Lugosi and Lon Chaney scaring hell out of everybody with a Fox Studio horror film called *Frankenstein Meets the Wolf Man.* Even behind prison bars the ex-convict had never had such horrendous dreams.

Then along the parkways to his own Lon Guyland home, to luxurious Fox Hall, adjoining the Woodmere Golf Club where nobody had then (nor has to this day) thrice made a hole in one. Nobody except this stickball player with the withered left arm.

Missing from Fox Hall and from their Park Avenue apartment were the art treasures that Mrs. Fox had acquired in Europe when she was shopping for large paintings for the ornate marbled lobbies of her husband's palaces in Atlanta, Detroit, St. Louis, San Francisco.

In the bleak previous December she had sold fifty-two paintings at the Jay Gould home at 579 Fifth Avenue for a total of only $39,025, including Gainsboroughs, Van Dycks, Tintorettos and Murillos. "Madonna and Child with Saints" by Peter Paul Rubens was sold for a mere $4,000, and his "St. Mark" and "St. Luke" went for a thousand dollars each.

Before his personal bankruptcy, Fox had set up for his wife and daughters the All-Continent Corporation, a holding company for stocks, bonds, patents, real estate and other valuables. Now Mrs. Fox and the family lawyer Benjamin Reass told him that this nest egg was being threatened.

Reposing in this corporate catch-all were leases to priceless real estate on both sides of Sixth Avenue which Fox had bought when the Rockefellers were assembling acreage for Rockefeller Center. His wily pint-sized A. C. Blumenthal had ferreted out for their Foxthal Corporation the southeast corner of 49th Street and Sixth Avenue and the northeast corner of 50th so that the masters of inherited wealth would have to buy his leases. But he outpriced himself, and Rockefeller architects revised their plans for the main entrance to the sixty-five-story RCA Building to nose west between Fox earmuffs.

These leases, along with one for a large plot bisecting the block west of Sixth Avenue behind the Roxy Theatre, were also in the grouch bag of these ladies, and it looked as if their husband and father had made sound provisions for a life of luxury.

But Time, as Virginia Cross philosophized in *Life's Shop Window*, the very first novel bought by Mrs. Fox for her husband's very first feature production in 1912, "has stolen up from behind us and taken the money from our hand: strength, health, beauty, youth, the biggest coin of all, has been snatched from us and we can buy nothing . . . only a few sweepings and remnants."

Whatever may have been the Fox meditations in his prison cell can only be surmised, but he seems to have decided to put in another appearance in life's shop window. Just a year after his parole, fourteen years after he had agreed with Harley Clarke to stay out of the film business for five years, he opened a small office on Fifth Avenue. It was April, 1944. He had only a secretary to help him. He was just five blocks from his former Roxy offices, with the ornate lounge, private dining room, steam room and massage table.

The only newspaper he read regularly was the *Times*, and on April 9, 1944, he told Thomas A. Pryor, when that *Times* movie specialist called at the office with its worn rented desk and three chairs:

"Now there is nothing to stop me from putting my name on a new company. I started with nothing and I'm not afraid to try again. Imagination and courage are still the essential elements for success in this business."

Fifteen years after he had announced his global plans for the next twenty-five years, he proclaimed, at the age of sixty-five, that he had taken an option on a 1,500-acre tract in Los Angeles where he would build a studio.

"Who knows what kind of entertainment people will want next year or two years from now? Personally I anticipate great changes not only in subject matter but in production techniques."

(This was nine years before his old company would embrace CinemaScope to compete with Cinerama.)

He said that he would again organize a system of exchanges to sell the pictures that he would produce in which he would give directors, stars and writers participation in the profits.

This would, of course, take money, and he had lost his. Would the bankers forget and forgive? Would the octopus retract its suctorial arms? Would Wall Street underwriters recognize the long-range vision of the formula that has made United Artists the hottest distributor in the world today?

What good Samaritan would lend a hand on the comeback trail?

The masters of Hollywood answered with the same aloof cynicism that they employed toward David Wark Griffith, whose creative innovations had presented them with the close-up, flashback, dissolve and fade:

"What have you done for me lately?"

His scrotum now.

21

CHAIRMAN SCHENCK

Time goes, you say? Ah, no! Alas, Time stays, we go.

—AUSTIN DOBSON

JOSEPH M. SCHENCK was an international playboy, a hedonist, a gambler operating gaming establishments in Mexico, the peer of Hollywood producers and their trusted bagman. Everybody loved Joe, including George Jessel, toastmaster general, who also loved Norma Talmadge so much that he married her after she divorced Schenck.

He was born in Rybinsk, Russia, on Christmas, 1882, and was brought by his parents to the United States along with the younger brother Nicholas. The Schenck boys grew up on the lower east side of New York, where they had a talented neighbor and friend named Isadore Baline, born in Russia May 11, 1888.

Baline got a job as a singing waiter in a Bowery saloon, where he jazzed tunes on the untuned piano, one of which he called "Alexander's Ragtime Band." As a rookie in World War I he wrote "Oh, How I Hate to Get Up in the Morning," and because of him they dream of a white Christmas even in sunny Rio de Janeiro. The composer publishes his own songs as president of Irving Berlin Music Corporation.

In 1954 Chairman Schenck was able to give his old pal employment writing three new songs to go into a wide-screen color picture featuring his all-time hits "Alexander's Ragtime Band," and "A Pretty Girl Is Like a Melody." In this colorful pasticcio Ethel Merman belted out Berlin's titular message "There's No Business Like Show Business." And of course there isn't.

The Schenck boys got jobs as errand boys in a drug store, studied pharmacy and soon were able to buy and operate two drug stores, one of them at Fort George, at the northern tip of Manhattan, where young people used to stroll and look across the Harlem River at The Bronx.

All this free promenading alerted the Schenck brothers to install a roller coaster and some other rides, which developed into Paradise Park. That put the Schencks into Show Biz.

After four years on Washington Heights they moved across the Hudson to the much larger Palisades Park. To swing that deal they acquired a partner named Marcus Loew, who owned a dozen vaudeville and film theatres.

The Schencks had acquired a theatre in nearby Hoboken and another in New Rochelle, which they threw in with their partner to establish Loew Consolidated Enterprises in 1910. These young go-getters helped Loew expand until 1919 in Delaware they got together to form Loew's, Incorporated, which owned or controlled fifty-six theatres. Nicholas Schenck became general manager of all the Loew enterprises.

Later they expanded to merge with Samuel Goldwyn and Louis B. Mayer and Metro Pictures, and, when Marcus Loew died in 1927, Nicholas Schenck was elected president of Loew's, Inc., and of Metro-Goldwyn-Mayer.

But running theatres was just booking and bookkeeping compared to producing, and Joseph Schenck turned to independent production during World War I. His enormously successful pictures starred Constance and Norma Talmadge (whom he married), Buster Keaton and Fatty Arbuckle, whose playboy orgy cost Schenck many millions.

In that 1920 era before electrical ice cubes, room service supplied chopped ice, which, when impacted to cool a hot babe during a drunken orgy, proved fatal to Virginia Rappe in Arbuckle's suite in a San Francisco hotel.

With two unreleased pictures starring his fat playboy, Schenck lost all his production cost and potential profits, because public condemnation prevented theatres from showing the pictures.

So great was the public uproar that William Fox took the initiative, with the approval of Zukor and Loew and other company presidents, in sending Saul Rogers to Washington to negotiate with the postmaster general in the cabinet of Warren Gamaliel Harding.

William Harrison Hays had been chairman of the Republican National Committee which elected President Harding, and Hays was privy to the then undisclosed Harding scandals. After some soul searching, the Presbyterian elder from Sullivan, Indiana, decided to quadruple his government salary and to become the first Czar of the Movies. His incidental expenses of $50,000 annually were considerably greater than the post office stipend.

Hays worked with Martin Quigley, a Knight of Malta, and with the Reverend Father Daniel A. Lord, S.J., in creating a Code of Morals which was rigorously enforced until 1945, when the handsome profile of Eric Allen

Johnston nosed Hays out as czar, and enforcement relaxed.

What price Valenti, now that X marks the dirt spot in the new classification code of the Motion Picture Association of America?

The skulduggery that went on during the Hays era was enough to test the stamina of the shrewdest politician and the ethics of a Presbyterian elder. In 1921, the bartender in a Chicago house of prostitution was sent to the penitentiary for perjury and pandering after the sudden death of his employer, Jack Zuta. After Willie Bioff got out of stir, Tom Maloy, business agent of Chicago local 110 of the International Association of Theatrical Stage Employees, was murdered in February, 1935. That provided an opening for George E. Browne, who took over the union with Bioff as enforcer, he having impeccable references from gangsters Lucky Luciano, Lepke Buchalter, Longey Zwillman and Frank Costello.

Threatening to bomb theatres, these goons were soon extorting more money than they could make as pimps, and before long stagehands, projectionists and cameramen discovered that their union membership gave them powerful protection. It was only naïve outlanders like my brother Earl who thought he could direct a Fox Movietone short in the Loop without local help, which he declined when offered. Within the hour he had a personal visit from Willie Bioff, who dressed him down as a fresh punk and warned that, if he wanted to take his pretty face and body back to New York without mutilation, he had better put six Bioff men on the payroll instanter. He did, after being beaten and dropped in an alley.

With that precedent I immediately hired a dozen stand-by technicians when I arrived in 1933 with a full Hollywood crew to produce a Chicago World's Fair sequence for my RKO feature *The Silver Streak,* starring the world's first diesel-powered, stainless steel streamlined railroad passenger train.

With Chicago so well organized that it could be left to underlings, Bioff and Browne decided that the important money in labor racketeering was in Hollywood, and they moved west to get into the big time.

During prohibition, Joseph M. Schenck, in partnership with the governor of Baja California, was one of the operators of the enormously successful casino, hotel and race track at Agua Caliente, and in those days practically everybody from the studios made weekend excursions across the Rio Grande. Schenck loved to gamble and one night dropped $30,905 gracefully in a poker session with Harpo Marx, but when he caught an unemployed vaudeville comedian dealing from the bottom of the deck the outraged producer gave him twenty-four hours to get out of California, and the comic flew to New York the next day and never returned.

With sound typecasting, the association of Hollywood producers unanimously decided that Schenck was best equipped to deal with Bioff and Browne, who had already convinced the officers and some members of all Hollywood theatrical unions that they needed protection from the tycoons who ran the motion picture industry. To keep the studios operating without strikes, to control projectionists from coast to coast so that their demands for wage increases were minimal, to stifle hotheads ready to drop stink bombs into theatres, to provide fire protection, surely these services were valuable, say about $50,000 a year from each of the eight big companies?

Possibly because some of the industry leaders were

themselves vulnerable with tax and bankruptcy and other irregularities, they decided to submit to blackmail and extortion instead of calling in a Thomas E. Dewey to defy these criminals and send them back to the penitentiary. Possibly they were so hypnotized with the menace of Edward G. Robinson and other Warner gangsters that their dream world became a terrifying reality. At any rate they asked Joe to work out the best deal he could and appointed him their official undercover bagman.

Schenck proceeded to give the boys what they wanted, which included many fringe benefits, and enlisted the help of his nephew Arthur Stebbins, who handled most of the insurance for the Schenck companies. More than a million dollars was passed along to Bioff and Browne by Schenck and Stebbins and whether they kept it all or shared it with international officers will never be known, for even at this late date one does not ask questions of or pass aspersions on top labor leaders.

Goons to the left of him, G-men to the right, poor Schenck was trapped in as nasty a mess as ever sucked earlier mastodons into the La Brea tar pits. Stuck, tarred and sinking, good old Joe could never work himself free.

Schenck and Stebbins were warned by Bioff that "you can't squawk or tell anybody about this deal. We ourselves will string along with you but our people never stand for anyone revealing anything harmful."

But gradually what was an industry secret began leaking out and some IATSE men risked their jobs and lives to explain what was going on to Arthur Unger, editor of *Daily Variety,* who had the courage to finger B&B.

Westbrook Pegler, snooping around Hollywood, dug up data for an explosive series on labor racketeering that won him a Pulitzer prize.

As a result of these disclosures, Bioff and Browne were arrested. Schenck testified at their trial that he and other executives had a responsibility to stockholders to protect their investments, and that he had no choice except to go along with the extortionists because "in labor matters and other things they were running matters by force and fear and intimidation, and that there was no limit to which they would not go if people did not do what they wanted."

In his testimony Bioff embarrassed Schenck by revealing that Schenck had made a gift of $200,000 to an investigator for a congressional committee probing bankruptcies of Fox, Paramount and RKO theatres. Other testimony threw searing backlighting on the mores and ethics of the hierarchy, cutting to extreme close-ups of Schenck.

Bioff and Browne and five other defendants were found guilty of conspiracy and extortion and were sentenced to ten years in the penitentiary. For Schenck it was purgatory.

How do accountants and insurance men and personal representatives separate legit from illegitimate, how pass around an undercover million dollars so that it looks kosher?

Soon the inexorable income tax collectors, who eventually catch up with the good guys like Joe and the bad guys like Al Capone, closed in on him, and Schenck and his co-defendant, Joseph H. Moskowitz, had a long jury trial in New York Federal Court. Schenck admitted that he had lied when in a previous trial he testified that a $100,000 payment was a loan to Bioff, and now the pimp Bioff and the payoff bagman Schenck were both officially branded perjurers.

According to Moskowitz, treasurer of Twentieth Century Productions, it had cost his old friend and employer $89,000 in business expenses to earn a 1937 salary of $117,000. As Judge Moscowitz (with a c) looked down from his bench on Joseph the k, the defendant tried to justify income tax deductions such as these:

1. $130 to fly Schenck's personal masseuse from California to New York.

2. $209 for insurance for the motor car of a girl friend.

3. $40,000 for the cost of operating the Schenck yacht, for which he had, according to the T-men, collected $25,000 rental for use by Twentieth Century-Fox.

4. $53 for a mattress for his sister-in-law, Mrs. Nicholas M. Schenck, wife of the president of Loew's, Inc., whose annual salary and bonus were in excess of $250,000, or enough to buy a mattress stuffed with ermine.

United States Attorney Mattias F. Correa told the jury that he had not been able to discover the source of the $100,000 in a paper bag which Schenck had deposited in the Bank of America (of which he was a director) one day in 1937 to pay off a loan, but assumed that it was related to a disputed payment which Bioff had sworn was not a loan.

In his summation, Correa told the jury that their verdict would show "whether there is a premium on wealth and power or whether downright fraud will be stamped out."

After ten weeks of testimony the jury of ten men and two women found both defendants guilty of three counts of tax evasion and one of conspiracy, and Judge Moscowitz sentenced Schenck to the federal prison in Danbury, Connecticut. There he served four months and five days.

But the judge spared Moskowitz from the penitentiary,

letting him off with a fine, and he returned to his production activities at Twentieth Century-Fox.

When Schenck was released from prison he returned to the studio as chairman of the board, and was granted a full pardon by President Harry S. Truman in 1945.

In 1949 when Schenck attempted to resign, the board refused to accept his resignation, and such directors as Robert Lehman, Seton Porter and Daniel O. Hastings agreed that he was indispensable. Schenck remained as executive producer until February 27, 1953.

When he died October 22, 1961, Spyros Skouras, in Temple Emanu-El, on Fifth Avenue in New York, said in his eulogy:

"In the history of the motion picture industry Joseph M. Schenck was a giant. The quality of his greatness was characterized first of all by his innate humanity, his love of justice and his willingness to help the underdog, with no thought of self. Though his rise in our industry was meteoric, his philosophic and humanitarian activities kept pace with it and he leaves a memory of service and devotion to an industry which owes him so much.

"Joe Schenck was just and kind to all with whom he came in contact. During his chairmanship of the board of Twentieth Century-Fox the company reached the acme of success."

22

NINETEENTH CENTURY FOX

It is well for the world that in most of us, by the age of thirty, the character has set like plaster, and will never soften again.

—WILLIAM JAMES, *Psychology*

AMONG the early pioneers, William Fox was not a lovable character, like Uncle Carl Laemmle or Joe Schenck.

He was no respecter of The Establishment and seemed to take delight in annoying the Rockefellers, as when he bought corner plots on Sixth Avenue at 49th and 50th streets, and that act of effrontery forced the west facade of the huge RCA building into the middle, its giant toes stepped on by two midgets.

And who was this immigrant who, in our glorious land of opportunity, defied the third generation of inherited wealth?

First-born of Orthodox parents Anna Freid and Michael Fuchs who, back in Tulcheva, Hungary, used to be an important citizen, with the tools and skills for pulling teeth. But here in the New York ghetto he was reduced to cooking stove blacking on the kitchen stove that heated the Stanton Street tenement next to the Sheriff Street public school attended from the age of six by the Fuchs, or Fox, children.

When he was nine, Will peddled the stove polish for five cents a can. When he was eleven he sold umbrellas on rainy days and nights. When he was thirteen, and pretending to be sixteen, he had advanced to foreman over a dozen men and boys cutting and sewing linings in coats.

To get to his bar mitzvah he had to lie and pretend to be sick, because puberty does not often catch up with a foreman.

From the toilet downstairs on Stanton Street he carried buckets of water to the kitchen, where the diapers were washed and dried for the dozen babies that arrived. But only the strongest lived, as nature demonstrated her formula for the survival of the fittest.

The dutiful father sent his sons to *cheder* to learn Hebrew and German and religion, and Jehovah left his message with the boy who scrounged for bones and scraps of meat to feed his younger siblings.

When, aged fifty-three, he was baring his soul to Upton Sinclair and recalling his boyhood struggles, Fox told Sinclair about the kosher butcher who "trusted little Will for meat and how little Will promised to repay him by taking care of him in his old age, and carried out that promise. After telling me this story, the grown-up Will added: 'Do you mean to tell me that God didn't give the butcher the idea to give me meat because He knew that he was going to be taken care of? That was God's way.' "

As we attempt to follow the story line devised by the Master Dramatist, we wonder how Fox script writers can hope to top the drama of the boy from Tulcheva. In 1927 he sent Fox newsreel cameramen to record the ancestral scenes, but he never visited his birthplace. He had little time for sentiment, with his demonic drive, night and day, to outsmart the competition and to dominate the world of motion pictures.

A great showman, a gambler who played the longest of shots, a fighter who recognized no Marquis of Queensberry rules, but was he a great man? It all depends on the point of view, as Orson Welles demonstrated when his camera probed the people who knew his *Citizen Kane;* as biographers found when they tried to understand the complex personalities of William Randolph Hearst or Howard Hughes.

His wife and two daughters adored him, and this matriarchy was the court of last resort in the Fox household. His two sons-in-law, divorced by Mona and Belle, were less enthusiastic when they were literary agents in Hollywood and I was story editor at the Paramount studio.

In the five years that I worked for Fox I never encountered him in an ugly mood, but Roxy and others shuddered at personal contacts with him. Once when he summoned me I caught a Tenth Avenue cinder in my eye (compliments of Consolidated Edison soft coal) and was blinking when I arrived. He whisked out a handkerchief, pried my eyelid open and removed the irritation.

He wore white socks and that has been held against him by some Ivy League bankers and lawyers, but the skin of his feet was as tender as his hide was thick, and he had the courage to wear what was therapeutically right.

His humor was primitive. Once when he called me in to give Roxy hell and pass along word as to what the new picture would be, I was wearing a red necktie and he flicked it out, commenting, "What's the matter, boy? Got a nosebleed?"

When I went to work for him, he told me that if he

never saw his picture in print again it would be all right with him. "This mug of mine will never sell any tickets, so just concentrate on getting the stars into magazines and newspapers, and forget about me."

But if his ego was not nourished by photographs, it was in full bloom in 1933. "I always bragged of the fact that no second of those contained in the twenty-four hours ever passed but that the name of William Fox was on the screen, being exhibited in some theatre in some part of the world.

"I knew the condition of every nation we traded with. No question could arise that by the push of a button could not be answered in the extensive files that I had adjoining my office. I had it completely systematized, so that I knew every move that was made throughout the organization.

"For more than thirty years I avoided carrying a watch. I never wanted to know what time it was. My day ended when my day's work was completed. Again and again I didn't go to bed at all during the twenty-four hours. There was work to do. I was working not only for myself but to help others. I had an ambition to build this monumental institution.

"It was always a charge that the Fox organization was a one-man organization. That was never said as a compliment to me, but a criticism. They were right when they said that. It is a fact that, if all the executives of the organization gathered to continue the business in case I died or became disabled, they would have had a problem on their hands. If they had produced the knowledge that each had and pieced it all together, they wouldn't have understood that which was continually being generated in my brain."

His ego was nourished by rebuffs. When he was the last

boy chosen for street games, desperation drove him to practice so that with his one good arm he could shoot better stickball than those who rejected him. When his employer did not appreciate him he found another employer who did—himself.

"It may be that my old employer was right when he said that I wasn't worth $17 a week. His name is Edmund Rothschild and he is a banker now and has, on occasion, extended me a line of credit at the Chelsea bank as high as $250,000," Fox recalled in 1933.

In 1928 he carried life insurance totaling $6,400,000 and told me: "I think I can say that if nobody else grieves my passing I can at least depend upon the president of every large insurance company in the world."

The inheritors of his largess, the president who succeeded him in the operation of the Fox enterprises, depending upon their own origins and cultures, hated him, tolerated him, were embarrassed by him or ignored him.

After more than a year in Doctors Hospital, overlooking Gracie Mansion, home of New York's mayors, William Fox died on May 8, 1952, from a complication of diseases. At the Temple Emanu-El on Fifth Avenue there was no eulogy from leaders of the industry he had helped create, but on the day of his funeral at Cypress Hills Cemetery a full-page advertisement appeared in the trade papers expressing just the right note of restrained corporate grief:

Twentieth Century-Fox bows in grieving tribute to one of the outstanding pioneers of the industry—*WILLIAM FOX*—and the early founder of the company which still bears his name.

WILLIAM FOX was one of the creative influences in this industry and in the fields of production and exhibition, in helping to bring sound on film to motion picture theatres and in establishing the newsreel with sound.

His daring, initiative and courage enabled him to make a signal contribution to the growth and development of the motion picture industry.

From the beginnings of his career he engaged in the production of films of magnitude and scope and blazed a trail for the industry in providing boxoffice attractions of wide popular appeal. He was truly a pioneer in foreseeing the present status of the screen as a medium of popular entertainment.

Those who knew him best will long mourn his passing.

As Mark Antony did not remark until the words were put in his mouth fifteen centuries later by an Elizabethan writer:

> "The evil that men do lives after them;
> The good is oft interred with their bones."

So let it be, and vice versa, with William Fox.

23

TWO DECADES OF SKOURAS

*The Old Guard in Hollywood no longer knows
what the hell is going on.*

—DAVID NEWMAN AND ROBERT BENTON
AUTHORS OF *Bonnie and Clyde*

BEFORE the United States Department of Justice
ordered producer-distributors to divest themselves of
their theatres, the 470 theatres of the Wesco Corporation
had been contributing about half the earnings of Fox
Film Corporation. If these theatres averaged a profit of a
thousand a week, this added around half a million dollars
a week to the revenues of Fox Film Corporation. But in
times of depression similar weekly losses could be disastrous, and on February 28, 1933, in the final weeks of the
Hoover Administration, Wesco Corporation was plunged
into bankruptcy, and the film company was out $5,113,-
965.40 advanced to Wesco plus $2,744,530.88 advanced to
Fox West Coast Theatres.

Charles Skouras was appointed receiver, and he and his
younger brothers Spyros and George cut operating expenses to the last postage stamp and paper clip as they
called personally on each theatre manager, in many cases
cutting his salary in half.

"Just call me Charlie," said the amiable slasher, and
many managers resigned, not calling him Charlie.

The Skouras brothers had learned the hard way how to run theatres in St. Louis, where in 1929 the Skouras Brothers Enterprises and the St. Louis Amusement Company had gone into bankruptcy with liabilities of $5,086,-410 against assets of $342,462 realized by the referee.

From their start in 1914 with one nickelodeon, acquired with their pooled savings of $4,000 earned as busboys and waiters in the Planters and Jefferson Hotels, they worked night and day, saved their money, borrowed and expanded, until in 1926 they owned thirty-seven St. Louis theatres, with the big new Ambassador as their flagship.

When Spyros was elected president of Twentieth Century-Fox in April, 1942, he had many favorable factors going for him, including the Chase Bank, cozy nepotism and two valuable studios, the one in Westwood being the only studio designed and built for sound. His brother Charles then operated about seven hundred theatres west of Kansas City and Milwaukee, and George operated several hundred theatres east of the Mississippi, and what was good for Charlie and George was also good for Spyros.

He had the astute inside advice of the chairman of the board headquartered at the studio, Joseph M. Schenck, who in 1935 had organized Twentieth Century productions with Darryl F. Zanuck. Because of his close personal and financial relationship with Nicholas M. Schenck, president of Loew's Inc., the chairman was able to make favorable deals for stars under contract to MGM, and what was good for Joe was good for Nick. Twentieth Century also had William Goetz as an investor, with money supplied by his father-in-law Louis B. Mayer, so that the sometimes quarreling Nicholas Schenck and Vice President Mayer each had self-interest in the advancement of Twentieth Century Productions.

More than a year after William Fox in 1928 had announced the abandonment of all silent picture production, Joe Schenck asserted: "Talking doesn't belong in pictures. I don't think people will want talking pictures long" and "It is my personal opinion that silent pictures will never be eliminated." But now Joe Schenck was in the saddle at Movietone City, where the greatest personal asset was Zanuck, the wonder boy from Wahoo, Nebraska. Zanuck after leaving Warner Brothers in 1933 had produced such hits as *The Bowery, Moulin Rouge, The House of Rothschild, Clive of India, The Mighty Barnum, Folies Bergeres* and *Les Miserables.*

After the Twentieth Century-Fox merger in 1953 Zanuck turned out a product that resulted in profits for 1942 and 1943 of ten million dollars for each of those years and more than twelve and a half million for 1944 and 1945. In 1946 the company's profits soared to an all-time high of $22,619,534, and the stock peaked at 63⅞.

With a loan that year of $20,000,000 from Chase National Bank, the Bank of America and Metropolitan Life, Twentieth Century-Fox (Spyros, president) retired for $7,415,000 all of the preferred stock held by executives of National Theatres (Charles, president; Spyros, chairman of the board of National Theatres Amusement Co., Inc.) .

In 1937, 1944 and 1950 Zanuck's associates in the Motion Picture Academy of Arts and Sciences voted him the Irving Thalberg award for outstanding production.

Net profits for 1948 and 1949 were above twelve million; in 1950, nine and a half million; in 1951, four million. This decline in profits worried Fox stockholders, and in April, 1953, Charles Green organized a committee of dissidents to campaign for proxies to oust the Skouras management. Green complained that common stock was selling substantially below book value and suggested that the corporation should buy in its own stock and so enhance the value of remaining shares, following the examples of Paramount and Warner Brothers.

Green also charged that up to $20,000,000 was being spent in the experimental development of Eidophor, a Swiss system of large-screen television projection for theatres, first announced in the 1950 annual report. After three years (also up to now) Eidophor was not ready for use in theatres.

In a letter to stockholders, dated April 21, 1953, President Skouras replied:

"I have spent 40 years in the motion picture industry—22 years of which have been in your company because I served 11 years with your former subsidiary, National Theatres, and have been your president for 11 years. I think I may be permitted to say that I understand the motion picture industry and its problems and the particular problems of this corporation.

"Since your present management took office, we have made a profit of $126,000,000 and paid out dividends of more than $68,000,000 in cash. Our investment and inventory has been increased by $35,655,000 without any additional financing."

Green offered to vote his stock for the election of Darryl F. Zanuck as president, but Zanuck declined that honor, being already overworked with the ulcerous responsibility of making daily million-dollar decisions. Within three years Zanuck became so fed up with this arduous task that he abandoned studio operations and moved to Europe to relax and make one or two pictures annually for Fox release.

The resilient Skouras, turning around on a centime in Switzerland, made an impetuous switch from the exasperating Eidophor to another Swiss invention, the squeeze lens which its inventor Dr. Henri Cretien had demonstrated at the 1939 World's Fair in New York, when Adolph Zukor passed it up for Paramount.

Earl Sponable, co-inventor with Theodore Case of Movietone, remembers how in the winter of 1952 he mentioned to Skouras that J. Arthur Rank in London now held an option on this Cretien invention which would soon expire. To confuse Rank, Skouras announced that Eidophor was ready for theatre installation and dispatched Sponable to Paris to await expiration of the Rank options.

Swooping down from an Alp on the amazed Dr. Cretien, Skouras and Sponable impounded his only anamorphic lens, made a quick deal for world-wide rights and flew back to California to launch CinemaScope.

So excited that his fractured English made him almost unintelligible, Skouras returned to the studio with the one squeeze lens in existence, and convinced Zanuck that they could make an impressive wide screen debut with *The Robe*, which had been before conventional color cameras for six weeks. Producer Frank Ross, who had been nursing along this novel by Lloyd C. Douglas for several years, was aghast when Zanuck showed him some squeeze lens footage and announced that he was going to scrap everything that Henry Koster had directed, and start shooting again with the new lens.

A special guard was set up night and day to keep an eye on the unique lens, and the first order of business each morning was to check the previous day's work to be sure there were no problems. Not until the picture was half over was a second lens delivered to the studio. In retrospect Darryl Zanuck told me, "This was the biggest God-damned gamble in screen history. Frank Ross was petrified as he visualized all his chances of participation going down the drain in excessive costs. In fact, his participation brought him a fortune."

Born of desperation from the impact of Cinerama, the failure of Eidophor, and stockholders nagging at declining profits due in part to the millions of people staying home to watch television, CinemaScope, in a photo finish, came just in time to make Skouras a hero and the savior of dying theatres. By installing his wide curved miracle mirror screens, exhibitors could retain their 35-millimeter projectors because the squeezed image on the film was projected to double size with a compensating expanding lens, giving it great economic advantages over the 3-cameras, 3-projectors, 2-streaks, extra-operators, fewer seats inherent in Cinerama. *The Robe,* which made its CinemaScope debut at the Roxy in New York September 16, 1953, set a world box office record for seven days of $364,428.

It was a proud moment of vindication when Skouras was able to announce to stockholders that 13,500 theatres in the United States and Canada and 7,000 additional world-wide had installed his system of curved screens and anamorphic lenses. The triumph of CinemaScope must be rated the greatest achievement of Spyros Skouras in his half century in the movies. It was Skouras alone among film executives, from Zukor to Rank, who saw and seized its potentials. Like an earlier Mediterranean adventurer into Gaul he could truly report: "I came, I saw, I conquered."

Unlike the founding father, President Skouras has

always aspired to statesmanship, and he reached the pinnacle when he was host to Nikita S. Khrushchev, the petulant premier who wanted only to go to Disneyland and had to settle (courtesy of State Department blundering, in my opinion) for Movietone City and a screening of *Can Can,* in which pelvic close-ups, in glorious CinemaScope, embarrassed his Georgian hausfrau first lady.

In a hands-across-the-Volga bear hug, these two world leaders, who had risen to unbelievable heights from humble origins, tried to top each other (through interpreters) about their poboy backgrounds.

(As Nunnally Johnson, studio wit and writer-director, commented on his birthplace in our own local Georgia: "Where I came from, *Tobacco Road* was considered the Country Club set.")

With the benign blessing of United States Ambassador (and Movie Czar) Eric Allen Johnston, this was the summit meeting of the year.

But luck ran out on President Skouras as it had on President Fox. With Zanuck in Europe, Joe Schenck in and out of prison, and nobody at the studio empowered to make daily decisions on contracts for actors and stories and to give the nod to package deals which agents brought in, Skouras in New York had to be consulted and, by the time he had conferred with his executive committee, many good deals were already lost to other studios. Such production delays and mounting confusions sent production into a tailspin.

"The difficult things we do immediately, the impossible takes a little longer," was one of the folksy Skouras maxims, and in 1962 he achieved the impossible, converting a Zanuck top profit of $22,619,534 into a Skouras deficit of $39,796,094.

But a compensating $43,000,000 popped out of the ground foresightedly provided by the founding father: Skouras sold 284 acres of studio property to the Aluminum Company of America, and leased back 75 acres until the year 2060 for an annual rental of one and a half million dollars, which is just five times the total purchase price of $300,000 for the original 108 acres.

Early in 1969, after the Aluminum Company of America had owned this Fox Studio acreage for less than a decade, the American Broadcasting Companies, Inc., leased four and a half acres for thirty years and are now building two movie theatres, a legitimate theatre, a restaurant, an office building, an arcade of stores and an underground garage. All of this new construction makes Century City a tremendous modern entertainment complex, jockeying for top position with Universal City just over Cahuenga Pass in North Hollywood.

Poor William Fox! He died before he ever knew the assets he sat on. Now only 4 per cent (or one small fairway) of the Westwood Golf Course he had so shrewdly purchased, brings in ten times as much rental as he paid for the whole original acreage.

Just how bad things were was hushed up as stock market researchers switched their recommendations from BUY to HOLD to SELL. Not until 1966, when resilient Fox was again leaping ahead, did President Darryl F. Zanuck admit to Mel Gussow in the *Herald Tribune* Sunday magazine *New York:*

"By 1962, Fox, under the presidency of Spyros Skouras, had worked its way to Rock Bottom, with Total Catastrophe and Ultimate Dissolution as its chief future prospects. . . . Every department was in bad shape. We had a split board, a conflict between Mr. Skouras and the board and a conflict between the production head and Mr. Skouras. And then the catastrophe of 'Cleopatra.' There was a drain on cash, a drain on everything. It was really chaos. I knew it was bad. . . . I didn't know how bad it was . . . the company was in immediate danger of 'evaporating.' "

Before he encountered rough going, Skouras is reported to have sent this telegram to an old crony exhibitor in St. Louis who was having financial difficulties: "No mariner ever distinguished himself in a smooth sea."

Q. What Fox mariner distinguished himself in a rough sea?

A. Darryl Francis Zanuck.

With an albatross around his neck, Skipper Skouras, in June, 1960, was still writing reports explaining some of his difficulties with Eidophor, "which has been the subject of enquiry on the part of some stockholders" because of a reputed research cost of around $20,000,000.

"As you know, we have been associated in the development of Eidophor—a large screen theatre color television system—for the past ten years. I am happy to say that a new holding corporation has been created for the Eidophor patents and various uses. Twentieth Century-Fox owns 50% of this company. The Swiss group consists of Gretag Limited of Zurich, Switzerland, an engineering firm wholly owned by Ciba—one of the largest pharmaceutical firms in Europe who owns the balance of the new holding corporation. They, in turn, associated themselves with Philips of Eindhoven, Holland, because they are in a better position to supply the electronics of the Eidophor system. We in America are also associated with the General Electric Company—working independently of the Swiss group on a parallel Eidophor project.

"Although we have had many Eidophor demonstrations in the past, using the sequential system—which requires at least a 15-megacycle band for short or long transmissions and AT&T had available only a 4-megacycle band—we have been unable to adopt the sequential system for commercial use. The expenses of equipping the country on a larger megacycle band would be prohibitive. Therefore, for the past two years, together with the above group, we have devoted ourselves to the development of the simultaneous system. This should operate successfully on an 8-megacycle band, which AT&T is now prepared to furnish."

Everything clear? Any questions?

24

OI TESSARES ADELPHOI SKOURA

Where two discourse, if the one's anger rise, the man who lets the contest fall is wise.

—EURIPIDES

IN Greece after World War I, a farm boy named Demetrius had his dreams of emigrating to America shattered when his father died and left him as the head of a family of three brothers and four sisters. But the Land of Opportunity, its outlines vague but always rosy in the setting sun, was such a compelling magnet that he thought perhaps he could offer his younger brothers as hostages to fortune in the United States. He sold sheep and crops to send his teen-age brothers to the city to learn English and arithmetic, and one by one shipped them off in the steerage to America to work and save and send back dollars for dowries for their sisters.

Demetrius dreamed his trans-Atlantic dreams and, when eventually they all came true, a family quarrel broke out, which is how St. Louis and Athens learned the details of the fabulous rise of Charles, Spyros and George Skouras, as dictated by Demetrius in Exhibit B, filed in the Circuit Court of the City of St. Louis in April, 1926, by his attorneys Lauchlin, Frumberg, Blodgett & Russel, in a petition *Skouras vs. Skouras,* which never came to trial because the visitor's permit of Demetrius expired.

Much to the relief of the younger brothers, the embarrassing greenhorn was deported.

What follows is unedited from court records:

My name is Demetrius Skouras. I am the plaintiff. The defendants are my brothers. We were all born in Skourohorion Elias, Greece.

When I was fifteen years old my father met with financial reverses which broke his spirit and destroyed his credit. Our family at that time consisted of my father and mother, four boys and four girls. The harsh necessities of time compelled me to quit school and to devote all my effort to bearing the burdens and responsibilities which my father previously had shouldered. My work consisted of cultivating, raising, and marketing crops, mostly raisin grapes, feeding and clothing the family, keeping us together, keeping my brothers and sisters in school, and reducing my father's indebtedness.

At the end of three years of constant labor I had accumulated a small sum of money which I invested in sheep. I also borrowed from a bank on my own credit the further sum of 2,000 drachmas. With these funds I rented land and went into the business of fattening and selling cattle. I gave the proceeds of my labor and the profits from my business to paying off my father's indebtedness, feeding and clothing the family, and educating the children. We lived under these conditions until I was 25 years old.

At this time my sister was to be married. By the custom of Greece it was necessary to provide her with a marriage portion. I was the only one able to do this, and I did it, in the amount of 8,000 drachmas.

Theda Bara as "Cleopatra" (1917) and Elizabeth Taylor in the color, wide-screen production (1963).

THE quaint photograph on the right represents the no-noes of the movies from 1922 to 1945, when Presbyterian elder Will H. Hays was czar. This hussy smoking a cigarette and baring her inside thigh while pointing a gun, was the personification of the screen sin which Will Hays battled for twenty-three years, assisted by Martin Quigley, Sr., trade paper publisher, and the Jesuit Father Daniel A. Lord, who helped write the production code of the Motion Picture Association.

When the handsome profile of Eric Allen Johnston nosed out the aging Hays, the new czar became much more permissive with fun in bed, while polishing platitudes to soothe his captive clubwomen.

In 1966, after Johnston's death in 1963, Jack Valenti, who had immortalized himself by announcing how well he slept while his employer Lyndon Baines Johnson was in the White House, became the third and current arbiter of screen morals. He may not be sleeping so well now that he has to justify bare breast nudity in *The Pawnbroker* (1965), obscenities in *Who's Afraid of Virginia Woolf?* (1966), big-nipple lesbianism in *The Killing of Sister George* (1968) and promiscuity in *Candy,* which was the 1968 Christmas saturation booking for the kiddies home from school.

"THOU SHALT NOT"

1 LAW DEFEATED
2 INSIDE OF THIGH
3 LACE LINGERIE
4 DEAD MAN
5 NARCOTICS
6 DRINKING
7 EXPOSED BOSOM
8 GAMBLING
9 POINTING GUN
10 TOMMY GUN

Richard & Darryl Zanuck

Glen Allvine with Czar Will Hays and President Herbert Hoover.

Barbra Streisand in "Hello Dolly!"

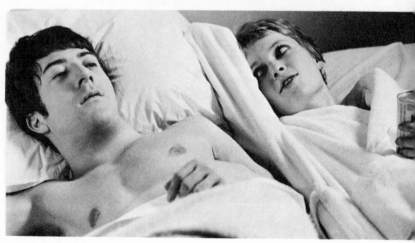

Dustin Hoffman and Mia Farrow as "John And Mary" have fun in bed.

Two or three years after my sister was married my brother Charlie completed his education, and I took him into business with me. He worked with me in the cultivation of crops, raising sheep and fattening cattle, for about a year, when he developed a rupture and was unable to work. I sent him to Athens, put him in the Evangelemos Hospital there, and had him operated on by the best surgeons in Greece. But he was unable to do further manual labor. I then sent him to Pergos to a private teacher to learn the English language, and maintained him there for about a year and a half. I also secured a position for Charlie (at 25 drachmas per month) so as to keep him away from bad associates after school.

I had heard of America as a land of opportunity, liberty, and justice. I felt that in that land was our destiny, and the place in the world God intended us to take. I told my brother Charlie so. I longed to go there. But I could not be spared. He could.

I told Charlie that I would sell enough of my cattle to pay his passage to the United States, that I would remain in Greece, and would continue to do the work, to look after and support the family, and to take care of the property as I had done in the past; that I would also send our other brothers to join him as soon as I could, and would finally come myself, if he would agree that everything that we all accumulated, the fruit of my labors in Greece as well as the fruit of his labors in America, should go into a common fund or pot, in which we four Skouras brothers should all have equal interests. He said that he would gladly agree and did agree. So we shook hands and parted. I went back to my hoe, and Charlie sailed away to seek our great perhaps.

Two or three days after Charlie left I sent Spyros to

the City of Pergos to learn English from the same teacher Charlie had gone to. Spyros remained there for about six months. I maintained him there. At the end of that time I took him out of this school and sent him to Patras and put him in a business school, where he took a general business course. I required him to specialize in the English language so as to prepare him for his going to the United States to join our brother Charlie.

I maintained Spyros at this business school for about two and one-half years. I furnished him 100 drachmas per month, and I secured a position for him in an office where he earned 25 drachmas per month. In this way he received business experience as well as business education.

After Spyros had been at this business school for about four months, I went to Patras. He met me at the station there and spoke of my shabby clothing. I told him of the struggle I had had to maintain the family, to furnish the money to send Charlie to the United States, to provide a dowry for our sisters, and to educate my brothers; that I had been compelled to send him the little money I had been able to put aside to buy some new clothes for myself; that it was more important that he dress as a gentleman than it was for me, and that I did not have enough money to properly clothe us both.

Spyros wept. He told me that everything he had in life, his food, his clothing, and his education, he owed solely to me, and that when he got to the United States he would dedicate the first ten years of his life to repaying me for what I had done for him. I then told him of the agreement that I had with Charlie; that that agreement was made for his benefit as well as ours; that I did not want him to dedicate ten years or any part of his life to me; that all I wanted was for him to become a party to the agreement between Charlie and me; that I was bettering myself by working and sacrificing as I had, in this, that the chances to make money in the United States were far greater than they were in Greece, and that by sending him and Charlie there I was taking a double bond of fortune. Spyros said that he would gladly become a party to that agreement; that everything that he accumulated in the United States should go into a common fund for our joint benefit, the benefit of the four Skouras brothers.

About three years after Charlie left for America I wrote and told him that Spyros was ready to go to the United States and asked him whether he could spare from our common fund which had been accumulated by his efforts the money for the journey. Charlie sent the money. Spyros spent it all in having his eyes treated. He wrote me so. I did not have the money to pay Spyros' transportation to the United States, so I sold fourteen of the sheep I had raised, took the money with me to Patras, and gave it to Spyros. That is the money which paid for his journey to America.

When I gave Spyros this money I told him that it was my understanding of our agreement that George and I would join him and Charlie in the United States as soon as we could. That in the meantime I would stay in Greece and take care of the family and property. That all the accumulations of that property, and all the results of my labor, were to go into a common fund or pot, and were to belong equally to us four brothers. That all that Charlie and Spyros acquired in the United States, and all that George and I might afterwards acquire in the United States, would also go into that same common fund, and that we four Skouras Brothers were to be equal owners in that common fund. I asked Spyros if that was his understanding of the agreement. Spyros said that my share in the common fund should be twice as great as that of any other brother, because it was I who had made the sacrifices, who had supported the family, who had borne the burdens and responsibilities, and who had supplied the opportunity. He said that he wanted me to agree that my share should be twice as much as that of the others. I told him no, that I did not want any more than any of my brothers, that all I wanted was that the original understanding be carried out. I asked him if he understood it as I had stated it. He said he did. I asked him if he agreed to it as I had stated it. He said he did.

I had a further talk with Spyros when he was leaving for the United States. In that talk I told him that I did not want him and Charlie to send money back to Greece unless I called for it. I told him I wanted them to invest all that they made in the United States, and whenever he saw an opportunity to make money, not to hesitate to borrow money and go in debt, and that I would back them up in doing so. Afterwards, on the train from New York to St. Louis on my first trip to the United States, Spyros told me that it was this advice and instruction that was responsible for our success in America.

About fifteen months after Spyros left for the United States, he and Charlie sent a ticket and a letter asking George to come and join them there. I then had a talk with George in which I told him of the understanding and agreement that existed between Charlie, Spyros, and myself. I told him that we three brothers had agreed that everything that we made and saved and accumulated, in Greece as in America, should go into a common fund and should belong equally to the brothers who became parties to the agreement and who contributed to the fund, and I asked George whether he would become a party to that agreement. George said that he would willingly become a party to the agreement, and that he would go to the United States and work as hard as he could to contribute as much as possible to our common fund. He thanked me for everything that I had done for him and for Charlie and Spyros, and said that I was the one who had made it possible for our brothers and himself to get their start in life.

After George had been in the United States about six months, my three brothers began to send money from America (aggregating about $800.00) for our common fund in Greece. They also wrote me from time to time telling me what they were doing to build up our joint estate in America, and their plans for the future. I put the money which they sent from America into our common fund in the name of Skouras Brothers, where I put also all of my own earnings and all of the profits from my business. With this money I bought the land I had been renting to fatten cattle on. I so reported to my brothers by letter. Spyros wrote in reply, congratulating me on what I had done, and stating that I alone had accomplished more for Skouras Brothers in Greece than the three of them had been able to accomplish for us in the United States up to that time.

In 1914 Spyros wrote me about going into the moving picture business, and about getting a theatre at Fourteenth and Market Streets to be known as the Olympic Theatre. I wrote and told him to go ahead. From this time on I constantly corresponded with my brothers, they asking and receiving my advice about our motion picture business in America, and I making reports to them of the progress of our affairs in Greece. In 1917 another sister was to get married. By the custom of our country it was necessary for us to provide her with a marriage fund. By correspondence we agreed to provide her with a fund of 14,000 drachmas. We further agreed that 11,000 drachmas of this fund should be contributed from our common fund in Greece, and 3,000 drachmas from our common fund in America. This was done.

In 1920 I received a letter from Spyros in which he told me that it was time for me to come to the United States, as it was understood I should do as soon as I was able to leave Greece. He told me that our business in America needed me, and that he thought that we should branch out and go into the importing business. I went to the United States and remained ten months. During all this time I was received by my three brothers as an equal owner in all of our American investments. I put in my time in St. Louis and lived at my brother Charlie's home. We were in almost constant conference over our varied interests, particularly the different theatrical enterprises in which our money was invested. They told me in detail about every property that we owned, how much was invested in each, how much was owed on each, and what each property was earning. During this stay in St. Louis whatever money I needed I drew from our common fund. My brothers all told me that whatever money I wanted should be drawn from that fund. All the money that I required during this period I got in this way. I also transferred money from our common fund in St. Louis to our common fund in Greece. This was done through George, as I had never had the time to learn English.

Among the properties which we owned at this time was a film exchange in the 3300 block on Locust Street. We were then operating under the name of Skouras Brothers.

Spyros told me that this name had been adopted because it indicated that our business was owned by us four brothers. The moneys which I transferred during this time from our St. Louis fund to our fund in Greece amounted to 35,000 drachmas. I transferred this money to purchase merchandise in Greece with which to start our importing business under the name of Skouras Brothers, Importers.

After ten months in St. Louis I returned to Greece, took care of our affairs there, and purchased olive oil, raisins, and other merchandise to use in our importing business in St. Louis. This took me about three months. I then came back to St. Louis and started our importing business which is still being conducted under the name of Skouras Brothers, Importers. My purchases for our importing business cost 120,000 drachmas. I paid on account the 35,000 drachmas transferred from St. Louis, as stated. The balance of 85,000 drachmas due on arrival of our importation in St. Louis we borrowed on the credit of Skouras Brothers. Spyros arranged the loan at the bank. As our raisins and olive oil were sold, we deposited the proceeds in the bank to the account of Skouras Brothers, Importers. On this occasion I remained in the United States about six months. During all this time I was recognized by my brothers as an equal owner with them in our common fund. All the money that I needed I drew from our common fund in St. Louis during the entire six months that I was here. During all this time I resided with my brother Spyros.

About March, 1922 I took with me from the common fund of Skouras Brothers about 75,000 drachmas, and went back to Greece, where I remained about a year and a half. Then I again purchased olive oil and raisins of the value of 180,000 drachmas and shipped them to the

United States. When the bill of lading on this importation reached St. Louis it was handled in the same way as before. I returned from Greece to St. Louis to market these importations, and remained here about a year and a half. During this time I resided with my brother George. When I had finished the business of selling our imported merchandise I devoted my time to our moving picture interests. I visited our moving picture houses in rotation, noted and checked the conduct of our employees, observed whether the paid admissions checked with the number of people actually present, and in general exercised the usual business diligence of an owner and proprietor in common with my brothers. Spyros requested me to come to the office the first thing every morning and I did so. He said that he wanted to talk to me daily, and from day to day, and to get my advice about the many questions continually coming up in connection with the management of our own theatres. He said that he thought that the best time to have such conferences was early in the morning. At all these conferences he referred to the theatres as our theatres, and treated me as an equal owner with himself. In the course of these conferences I told Spyros that what we ought to do was to put up a large theatre of our own at the most advantageous place in St. Louis; that our stock holdings in our various theatres amounted to about $1,500,000.00; that with this stock as collateral we could go to the president of some bank and make arrangements to borrow perhaps as much as $2,000,000.00; that with this money we could put up a large first-class theatre at the most advantageous point in St. Louis. I won Spyros' consent to this idea. I persuaded him to go to a banker (as he could speak English and I could not), and in this way secured through him an offer

from the bank to Skouras Brothers of the lot at the North-
west corner of Seventh and Locust Streets at the price of
$1,500,000.00, and a loan of $500,000.00 to be applied towards the building of the theatre. Spyros submitted this
offer of the bank to his three brothers as his joint associates. We all talked it over in the office of Skouras
Brothers, and instructed Spyros and Charlie to go back to
the bank the next day and to state that we accepted their
proposition as made. This they did. We further authorized them to put up all of our stock in Skouras Brothers
enterprises as collateral to secure the bank our joint debt
of $1,500,000.00 for the lot and $500,000.00 for the building loan. This, too, was done.

A few weeks after this deal had been closed we received
an offer to sell our location at Seventh and Locust Streets
at a profit of $500,000.00. We jointly debated this offer
and jointly rejected it. The same parties then offered to
lend us the money to put up on our lot an office building
with the theatre in it. This deal we eventually closed.

We held a number of meetings at which all four
brothers were present, at each of which we considered
one or more of the many propositions that were submitted
to put up an office building and theatre on our lot. We
debated the respective merits of these offers, and in the
end finally concurred. The project was started in accord-
ance with our determination, and the building is now in
process of construction. At this period we debated and
agreed that it was best for our joint interests for me to
make a trip to Greece and arrange for the importation of
some more merchandise.

I left St. Louis for Greece about April 14, 1925. Our
common fund, held in the name of Skouras Brothers in
St. Louis, supplied all my expenses. My brothers told me

not to hesitate to draw on our joint fund in St. Louis for whatever money I might need in Greece. It was agreed between us at the time of my departure that the next time I came back to the United States I would become a citizen and would remain here permanently.

On this trip I remained in Greece about five months, during which I purchased about 25,000 pounds of raisins and shipped them to St. Louis. I returned to the United States about October 5, 1925. On leaving Greece, I made application to the American consul, told him that I wanted to come here permanently, and told him that I wanted to become a citizen. He advised me that my admission was barred, because the quota that could come from Greece to the United States already had been filled.

On this account I had difficulty in getting into America. I was sent to Ellis Island and detained there. Spyros came to see me there, reported to me the condition of our affairs in St. Louis, and received my report on the condition of our affairs in Greece. He told me that our new theatre at Seventh and Locust Streets was going to make us a lot of money. As soon as I was released from Ellis Island we came to St. Louis together.

Shortly after my return to St. Louis my brothers asked my advice on the way in which our theatre business was being managed. I advised that the managers of our different theatres had too much authority to spend money; that we needed a check on expenditures; that I thought that George should devote his time to checking and approving every expenditure of every theatre before it was made, so as to insure economy. My brothers accepted this advice, and George is acting in that capacity today. My plan resulted in a saving for all of us of about $100,000.00 a year.

On my return to St. Louis this last time, I resumed my old duties of general supervision of our theatres. I have also continued the active management of our importing business. All the proceeds and profits of the importing business have gone into the common fund of Skouras Brothers, and have been deposited in the name of Skouras Brothers, Importers. I have not withdrawn or received any money for services either for managing the importing business or for general supervision of the theatres. My services have all been compensated by the increasing value of my one-fourth interest in the common fund of Skouras Brothers. In brief, I have been working for myself as well as my brothers, have found my compensation in the growth of my own property, and until recently have been recognized by my brothers as a full and equal owner of an undivided one-fourth interest in our common fund, on which I have heretofore been free to draw at such times and for such amount as I saw fit.

About two months ago my three brothers entered into a conspiracy among themselves and with each other to get rid of me, and to misappropriate to their own use my undivided one-fourth interest in our common fund. To accomplish this conspiracy they have employed ruffians to bump into me, to pick a quarrel with me, and to do me serious bodily injury. They have employed and incited a woman to endeavor to get me in a compromising position which would enable them to foment proceedings to have me deported as an undesirable alien. Here lately they have ordered me to quit learning the English language, and to go on back to Greece. They have wrongfully denied and repudiated our agreements creating our common fund, our many years of recognition of those agreements, full performance thereof on my part, full recognition of my right on their part, and my resulting one-fourth interest in the lands, leaseholds, stocks, bank accounts, moneys, and other property of Skouras Brothers in America, standing in the name of Skouras Brothers, but immediately under their control, because of the growth and conduct of our business as above stated, and because, on account of my ignorance of the English language, and on account of the fact that I have trusted implicitly in their integrity and their honor, I have allowed to remain subject to their individual control. All of our property in Greece is in the name of Skouras Brothers, the same as the property in this country, but as our contract is well known and understood in Greece, they are unable to dispossess me of my interest there, nor can I dispose of any of our property there without my brothers joining with me in the deed. Yet by their wrongful denial of my rights in our common fund in America, they have wrongfully dispossessed me of my interest in our common fund here in America, and have wrongfully appropriated the same to their own use, to my damage in the sum of $500,000.00, for which I ask judgment with costs.

For a second cause of action against defendants plaintiff alleges that he and the defendants are brothers, and are all natives of Greece; that heretofore, to-wit, about May, 1907, plaintiff entered into an agreement with the defendant Charles, in Greece, that plaintiff would provide the money to send Charles to the United States, would later send the other brothers there to join him, and would finally come himself, and would in the meantime educate, support, and clothe the other brothers, the parents, and the sisters of Charles, and would in general discharge all of the obligations of the four brothers to the members of their family, in consideration of which Charles agreed that he would work in America for the joint benefit of plaintiff, himself, and the other brothers who would later become parties to the agreement, and that everything that was accumulated by all of them, the fruit of plaintiff's labors in Greece as well as Charles' labors in America, should go into a common fund or pot in which the four Skouras brothers should all have equal interests.

About July, 1910, in Greece, the defendant Spyros agreed to become and did become a party to said agreement, and plaintiff agreed to and did send him to the United States, agreed to send George thereafter, agreed to come finally himself, and agreed that all that plaintiff had theretofore accumulated in Greece, and all that he might thereafter accumulate, should go into a common fund or pot for the benefit of the four Skouras brothers, plaintiff and defendants, in consideration of which Spyros agreed that he would do everything in his power to accumulate money and property in the United States, and that everything that he did thereafter accumulate should go into the same common fund or pot, and should be and become the joint property of plaintiff and defendants under the name of Skouras Brothers, share and share alike.

About September, 1911, in Greece, the defendant George agreed to become and did become a party to the said agreement, agreed to go to the United States and to work as hard as he could to accumulate money and property for the common fund, in consideration whereof plaintiff advanced him money for his expenses, admitted and received him into equal ownership in the common fund of Skouras Brothers in Greece, and his brothers Charles and Spyros received him into the Skouras Brothers partnership in America.

Thereafter plaintiff in all things duly and fully performed his obligations under said agreement, and contributed and furnished his money, labor, skill and advice, credit, and means, to the partnership of Skouras Brothers, and to the joint account of Skouras Brothers, and to the common fund of Skouras Brothers, and the defendants each did likewise, the plaintiff operating for the benefit of the partnership chiefly in Greece and the defendants operating in like manner in America, and each of the four brothers was received by the other three as an equal owner and proprietor in all the plans, projects, properties, accumulations, and enterprises of said Skouras Brothers.

That as a result of the joint planning, effort, enterprise, credit and means of said Skouras Brothers, the said Skouras Brothers accumulated divers and sundry property of great value in and about the City of St. Louis, the property listed on the schedule hereto attached and marked "Plaintiff's Exhibit A." Said properties are of aggregate value of, to-wit, $2,000,000.00. Title to some of them is held by the St. Louis Amusement Company, a corporation, in which Skouras Brothers own all the stock. Title to others is held by Skouras Brothers Enterprises, a corporation, in which Skouras Brothers own a majority or control of the stock. On account of plaintiff's absence in Greece, and his ignorance of the English language, he has permitted the defendants to have supervision and control of the corporate machinery of the corporations which hold the title to said properties of Skouras Brothers, and defendants, in abuse and breach of their said trust, have wrongfully suppressed and kept plaintiff's name from the records of said corporations, so that his one-fourth interest does not appear of record, and defendants are now wrongfully denying the existence of such interest, and are wrongfully attempting to cheat and defraud him of the whole thereof.

The properties listed on said Exhibit A are all real estate lying, being, and situate in the City and County of St. Louis, Missouri, and plaintiff's claim is for an undivided one-fourth interest in and to such real estate, subject to incumbrances of record, and also a one-fourth interest in the revenues of said properties, and in the stock of the corporations holding record title thereto. The defendants have wrongfully refused to account to the plaintiff for the revenues of said properties, all of which are income-producing, have produced large revenues in the past, and are now continuing, and in all likelihood will continue, to produce large revenues, but without a discovery and accounting plaintiff cannot tell either the detail or the aggregate thereof.

WHEREFORE plaintiff prays that he may be adjudged and decreed to be an equal owner with the defendants in and of the property described in said plaintiff's Exhibit A; that his ownership thereof may be decreed in such manner as will put it beyond the power of the defendants to alien or incumber the same; that to that end the defendants be required, by mandatory injunction if necessary, to cause title to such undivided one-fourth interest to be conveyed to plaintiff; that defendants be decreed to be accounting parties, and ordered to account to plaintiff in equity for all the income and revenues of all such said properties down to the date of the accounting; that plaintiff have leave to surcharge and falsify such account; that trial be had of the issues raised by defendants' statement of account, and by plaintiff's surcharges and falsification thereof, and that a money judgment be rendered in favor of plaintiff and against defendants for the sum to be found due on such accounting; that such money judgment be decreed a first and paramount lien on the three-fourths interest belonging to defendants in said property described on Exhibit A, and that plaintiff have such other and further relief as equity and good conscience may require.

25

TWENTIETH CENTURY-FOX

The stage but echoes back the public voice,
The drama's laws the drama's patrons give;
For we that live to please must please to live.

—SAMUEL JOHNSON

WHERE the Fox companies have pioneered with new inventions, all the other film companies have followed them, twice, and three times Fox has been shaken by Swiss-German patents that have slipped down from the Alps with the impact of an avalanche of melting snow.

In 1928 the Fox-Case patents inspired by Yale-Cornell researchers transformed the industry from silence to sound. In 1953 the Swiss CinemaScope precipitated wide screens. In 1933 the German Tri-Ergon patents gave William Fox his monopolistic interest in all the theatres in the Americas. And in 1950 Spyros Skouras embraced the Swiss Eidophor which dragged him down.

Alpine score: 2 hits, 1 error.

Apart from its technology, Twentieth Century-Fox Film Corporation today is what four men have made it: (1) William Fox; (2) Sidney Kent, who brought in Zanuck; (3) Spyros Skouras, whose management in two decades gave the company some good years and some disastrous ones; and (4) Darryl F. Zanuck, who twice delivered the company, in 1936 and 1962, from financial chaos.

Until Zanuck took over as president in August, 1962, its product and policies reflected the personality of Spyros Panigiotis Skouras. Being an exhibitor, he attempted to maintain a steady flow of product from factory to point of sale. Being an Orthodox Greek churchman, he held to high standards of screen morality and passed up some of the fast-buck sex bonanzas and the lurid product bookings that make West 42nd Street in New York a cesspool of cinematic filth in what *Variety* calls "Slime Square."

As Skouras explained to stockholders in 1960:

"We are not only a picture company but an institution of great social importance, and as such we must be constantly conscious of the great privilege and its consequent responsibilities. . . . A large number of our productions are designed for the family trade. These pictures have been and will be designed to appeal to all ages, of both sexes, but will have an especially great appeal to the youthful moviegoers in the United States and around the world. Creating good, clean entertainment for the youthful moviegoer makes good moral sense and therefore intelligent business practice. Today the young are the mainstay in patronage. . . . We consider it a great responsibility to provide the highest type of entertainment, a responsibility for the advancement of our society and a better world. . . . It is the objective of Twentieth Century-Fox to produce and distribute motion pictures of the highest quality which will enlighten, as well as entertain, and always reflect dignity and credit on the American people, in every quarter of the globe."

Occasionally, in his reports to stockholders, Skouras blamed "our production division" for losses (as if to negate responsibility for the basic business of the company) and noted, June 20, 1960, that "we expect two of our current productions to break even, and three pictures will show a loss."

Other divisions he praised:

1. Twentieth Fox Records, launched in 1958, which "has established itself in the industry."

2. KMSP-TV, an American Broadcasting Company affiliate in the Minneapolis-St. Paul area.

3. National Telefilm Associates, which in 1956 began selling fifty-two pre-1948 features in the United States, Cuba and Mexico, and which continued domestic syndication of old movies.

This is only token diversification compared to the spun-off Fox West Coast Theatres, now known as National General Corporation, which currently owns the Columbia Savings and Loan Association, with assets of $107 million; Mobile Rentals, manufacturing portable buildings on steel frames; the venerable book publishers, Grosset and Dunlap; Community Antenna TV stations in five states; and, on the wave of the future, the big-screen color system Talaria, being developed by General Electric to transmit by wire sports events and stage shows into film theatres and auditoriums.

It is not in the states but overseas, where the film company was able to expand without United States government restraint that Twentieth Century-Fox has flowered from the seeds planted by Winfield Sheehan just after World War I. What used to be known as the foreign department is now the envy of all other producer-distributors, with assets such as these:

1. Offices in sixty-six foreign markets.

2. One hundred hardtop and twenty-two drive-in theatres in Australia, plus five television stations.

3. Exclusive food concession in Melbourne's largest shopping center.

4. Forty-three theatres in New Zealand.

5. A South African complex including cinemas, stage theatres, a stadium, and the Boswell Wilkies circus traveling in its own train.

6. Theatre Caterers, Ltd., serving eighty-two theatres in southwest Africa and Rhodesia, with its Holiday Inn Catering Service bringing TV-type cooked foods and packaged orange juice to the local movie buffs.

7. Killarney Film Studios in South Africa.

8. A magazine *Stage and Screen.*

9. Films and equipment for theatres in Kenya, Uganda and Tanzania.

In 1969 President Zanuck sold back to the Schlesinger organization 80 theatres and related businesses in South Africa for a profit, after taxes, of $14,600,000. These properties had been bought from the Schlesingers in 1957 by President Skouras.

In the United States and Canada the company is self-contained for the production and processing of films for every purpose. In addition to the original twelve-acre Sunset and Western Studio, its seven stages now busy grinding out films for TV, and the main Westwood plant, the company owns 2,738 acres in a valley just thirty miles over the Malibu hills which are now being developed for production to phase out Westwood gradually under a program developed by the Stanford Research Institute.

Fox Movietone News, established 1928, is dead, technological victim of the Vision-by-Radio process that caused William Fox to start building 5,000-seat theatres, but its incomparable library of some 90,000,000 feet and its pioneering sound equipment are now part of the modernized Film Center, at 54th Street and Tenth Avenue, New York, equipped for everything required for the production of theatre features, TV commercials and documentaries, with modern mixing and recording equipment and optical facilities.

The original Deluxe Laboratories at 850 Tenth Avenue, New York, have been augmented by the purchase in 1964 of the General Film Laboratories in Hollywood, Chicago and Toronto, providing highly automated operation for control and precision printing of both color and black and white, negative and positive.

In 1967 the company paid $4,200,000 for the music publishing company of Bregmen, Vocco & Conn, to bolster Twentieth's long-time income from a 25 per cent interest in Robbins-Feist-Miller.

In 1969 a New York-based teleblurb production company, Wylde Films, was acquired for stock and cash, and its personnel is now contributing this highly specialized technique to the Fox conglomerate.

With all of these magnificent facilities, all the company has to do is to make entertaining and profitable pictures for theatres and television. So simple a goal; so complex a procedure.

Take *John Goldfarb, Please Come Home,* for instance. Whoever first read the novel by William Peter Blatty must have thought it hilarious, and it was only natural to engage the novelist to write the screenplay.

You get a top director, such as J. Lee Thompson, you sign up a name with international appeal, like Peter Ustinov, you undress the alluring Shirley MacLaine and turn her loose with the other girls in an oriental harem, you gag up the footballers in DeLuxe Color and Cinema-Scope, and you've got what they're crying for, world-wide.

But something went wrong, resulting in that saddest of phenomena, an overstuffed, unfunny comedy. I know with what anguish everybody involved must have reacted when the New York reviewers reported on the picture. Being only a paying auditor, I gave myself the luxury of composing another quotation ad, one of hundreds I had knocked out for earlier Fox pictures (see page 211).

Whoever gave the production nod to that two-million-dollar project was absolutely right on paper and yet somehow wrong on acetate film.

A cosmopolite now operating out of London, Mike Frankovich, former production head of Columbia Studio in Hollywood, is still groping, along with other harassed decision-makers, for the right formula. While welcoming outside producers in Hollywood, he did not give them free reign in United Artists fashion.

"It's simply the classic system of checks and balances," Frankovich explained. "I believe that the studio chief or the executive producer should be a strong sounding board to guide films along to more suitable paths. Total autonomy is not the answer."

As they analyzed box office statements and saw *Goldfarb* die and *Goldfinger* skyrocket, the Frankoviches and the Mirisches and the Hymans and the other top bananas made their global decisions and hoped for the best. These veterans of mass production well knew that in the United States more than half of our total population is under the age of twenty-five. While they were pondering how to cater to these groping adolescents, a new breed of filmmakers, out of TV and college, moved in, and are now taking long-shot chances on films not in the traditional mold.

"Don't you believe that all films should have a beginning, a middle and an end?" a student asked recently at a college seminar.

"Of course," he was told, "but not necessarily in that order."

In the great, orderly, mass-produced days of Mayer and Thalberg the world return on films outside the United States and Canada was about 35 per cent. Now the domestic and overseas markets are 50/50.

This 15 per cent differential, and the upsurge in Italian and British production, has affected Hollywood attitudes toward such quaint old bans as horizontal clinches and has stimulated more fun in bed. Some of the current on-screen nudity must be causing Elder Will Hays to do double nipups in his segregated Presbyterian heaven.

Although one of the most popular pictures of 1966 was Walt Disney's *Mary Poppins,* with world rentals of about fifty million dollars, so-called art houses in the United States did well with Italian, Swedish and other sexologies. Such art theatres attract audiences unknown in the cultural world of William Fox, and some of his former marginal theatres are now prospering with these foreign language imports.

The runaway financial success of Twentieth Century-Fox was *The Sound of Music,* which was brushed off as beautiful but corny by many reviewers, but the influence of New York film critics is minimal compared with the boys with by-lines on stage shows. Better a Zanuck than a Merrick be with thousands of box offices instead of just one, that can collect more than $115,000,000 globally.

Always ready to take a bow, presidents, vice presidents, general managers of production and individual producers and directors find it humiliating to take a slow boat to Australia, as literally happened to Joseph R. Vogel, 1963 president of MGM, who had to take the rap for *Mutiny on the Bounty,* which turned out sour, courtesy of Marlon Brando. This was the same man who in 1959 was acclaimed a hero and saved the company when he guessed right on *Ben Hur.* The industry hall of fame is strewed with fallen heroes who have made just one wrong guess.

26

TWENTY-FIRST CENTURY FOX

*Time has no divisions to mark its passage, there is
never a thunderstorm or blare of trumpets to announce the beginning of a new month or year.
Even when a new century begins it is only we
mortals who ring bells and fire off pistols.*

—THOMAS MANN

THE man who calls the shots at Twentieth Century-
Fox these days and nights did not want to be president, but had to accept the grueling responsibilities because Darryl Francis Zanuck and his family owned
117,305 shares of the common stock, which makes him by
far the largest stockholder.

July, 1962, marked the end of Zanuck's playboy days in
Europe, where pretty young things and relaxed personal
production occupied his days and nights, and it was the
beginning of his dynamic reconstruction of a declining
empire.

As an independent producer, financed and distributed
by Twentieth Century-Fox, he had filmed in Europe and
Africa some so-so pictures, not any of them in the same
class with his great productions in the days prior to 1956.

As a continental playboy he admits that he had been
drinking too much and relaxing too hard with nubile
babes, and he did not deny the prowess attributed to him
in a kiss-and-tell book by inamorata Juliette Greco.

All that had changed four years later when in his London hotel, away from the turmoil of Hollywood and New York, Zanuck relaxed on a confessional couch and talked candidly with Peter Evans, as reported in December, 1966, in the *London Express*.

As Evans described the interview: "It was New Year's Eve in New York, 1961. The temperature had fallen almost 10 degrees overnight and it was now 18 degrees Fahrenheit and the first snow of winter was about to come. The cold paralyzed the faces of the people on the streets and made them seem unfriendly and friendless as the black Cadillac moved patiently through the crawling cross-town traffic.

"In the back of the car, with his lawyer Arnold Grant, was Darryl F. Zanuck. It was a few minutes before ten o'clock in the morning, and already Zanuck was biting pretty good on his first cigar of the day.

" 'Darryl,' said Grant as the car arrived at the shabby, slum-like warehouse of a building on West 56th Street that is the headquarters of the most famous film company in the world, 20th Century-Fox, 'Darryl, let's keep it calm.'

"Zanuck removed his cigar, studied the ash for a moment, and said: 'Calm.' The ash didn't move and Grant hoped it was a good sign.

"The two men were going to see Spyros Panigiotis Skouras, the volatile Greek-born president of the company. Grant just hoped he could keep the tension out of the encounter. For although Skouras regarded Zanuck with something close to paternal affection, and Zanuck reciprocated with respect for the aging president, the two men were emotionally incompatible.

"Zanuck, after a 22-year reign as the arbitrary boss of

the powerful studio, had quit the company four years earlier to become an independent producer. But his recent record—with such pictures as 'Crack In The Mirror,' 'The Big Gamble,' 'Roots of Heaven'—was not impressive.

"But still Zanuck's record over the years was solid and now he was on the eve of shooting his most expensive and ambitious picture ever; the $8 million war epic 'The Longest Day.'

"Grant and Zanuck took the drafty hand-operated elevator to the third floor and walked down the corridor lined with the framed glossy portraits of past, present, dead and forgotten Fox stars. Past Betty Grable, Tyrone Power, Alice Faye to a door marked Office of the President.

"Skouras, a small, weighty, white-haired man with the kind of a face they would issue to ambitious Father Figures, came forward smiling. But predictably, within some 90 seconds, as the fur flies, Skouras had retreated behind his expanse of executive desk and was beginning to work over his amber worry beads.

"Zanuck was on his second cigar, jammed into his face and now occasionally jumping like the needle on a seismometer that knows something.

" 'From 10 o'clock until 12:30 the pair of them were fighting like hell as they always did,' Grant recalled later.

"What neither Skouras nor Zanuck knew then was the quiet strain, the hidden pressure, the other was under. At that time Skouras, then 68, was in some pain and was soon to undergo surgery. Further, and perhaps more painful to the proud old Greek, was the fact that he had just been given the secret estimated loss for 1961: a massive $22 million.

"It was a bad time, too, for Zanuck. His long association with Juliette Greco was over (he was to observe later

'I spent two years of my life trying to make her a star. When you're stuck on a girl you do a lot of stupid things.')

"So here they were, two of the most powerful, legendary but privately pressured men in the cinema industry, 'squabbling like children.'

" 'Finally I blew my stack,' said Grant. 'There was Skouras, now an old guy, sick, proud, unbending, niggling as hell and going around in circles while the company was sinking under him. And Darryl was drinking pretty heavily then; the edge was going.'

"So it was at 12:30 on Dec. 31, 1961, Arnold Grant stood up in the president's office and swore at the two men. The quick anger, coming from a cautious man of law, was as if somebody had suddenly blasphemed in the middle of a church service. Grant carefully packed his papers. Finally: 'You guys make me sick,' he said, his voice low key.

"Grant buttoned up his overcoat. 'Gentlemen,' he said, 'I'm sorry for you. Good day.' Arnold Grant walked out of the office of the president, down the corridor lined with the glossy smiles made with capped teeth and Vaselined lips.

"On that particular New Year's Eve in New York City the brilliant, prudent, sober lawyer 'got good and drunk.'

"But Zanuck didn't get drunk. Grant, perhaps not accidentally, had 'hit him where he lived' when he accused him of drinking too much. At first it angered Zanuck, then it worried him. He knew it was true. He was putting away a fair amount of the hard stuff since he left Hollywood in 1956."

The more he thought it over the more Zanuck realized that Grant was right, and he telephoned him from Paris to tell him so, and to report that he was off the laughing soup.

Meanwhile, back in California, Skouras stopped pro-

duction on *The Chapman Report* just ten days before
Richard Zanuck was to roll the Westwood cameras. This
was the last straw. Darryl Zanuck's only son Richard had
grown up in film business, and ever since graduating from
Leland Stanford had worked intimately with his father
on all his independent productions.

"I got mad," Zanuck pere admitted as his old Alma
Mater Warner Brothers picked up the "Chapman" script
and hired Richard to produce it.

But over in Rome there was no such easy solution for
the most expensive production in the history of films.
Cleopatra had gone from bad in London to worse, doubled
in hearts, in Rome.

The basic Skouras mistake had been in picking rainy
England for the shooting of a sunny Egyptian story, and
this climatic error was compounded with pneumonia from
which Elizabeth Taylor almost died. This was two and a
half million dollars down the drain when a new director
was hired to write at night and direct by day a fantastic
off-the-cuff operation that by 1962 had pyramided production costs to around thirty million dollars.

If the company in which he was the largest stockholder
was to be saved from liquidation, Zanuck realized that he
now needed Grant more than ever to give battle to Roosevelt's presidential adviser Samuel I. Rosenman, who had
come from Franklin to Spyros as a "responsible and impartial outsider."

On June 15, 1962, Zanuck and Grant went to work on
the Wall Streeters on the board, Robert Lehman, John L.
Loeb and Milton Gould, and eventually convinced them
that receivership and liquidation were inevitable unless
the man who had the most to lose had a free rein to save
his family investment.

These bankers, familiar with Procter & Gamble and other manufacturers, finally realized that nothing much, except some new packaging, had happened to Ivory Soap in half a century, and that what this film factory basically needed was a man to design, manufacture and package almost every week a new product chemically, physically and emotionally attractive to world-wide buyers. And here was Zanuck, top expert on product, pleading to sink or swim.

And so it was angrily debated, in the longest and stormiest board meeting since William Fox battled Wall Street bankers thirty-two years earlier, until finally Skouras, the second biggest stockholder, was kicked upstairs as chairman, and on July 25, 1962, Zanuck was elected president and chief operating officer.

Once in the saddle, Colonel Darryl Francis Zanuck rode off in all directions, attacking his corporate enemies. His slashing attacks were right out of *The Longest Day,* which was his European answer to Hollywood production, a picture that has given him a personal profit of more than three million dollars, as the biggest black-and-white blockbuster in the history of Fox production.

"We'll just have to adopt twenty-first century methods," he announced as he personally slashed away at the interminable footage of *Cleopatra.*

It was a good line, whatever its mystique, and it certainly got results, as Producer Zanuck fired Field Producer Walter Wanger; Director Zanuck relieved Writer-Director Joseph L. Mankiewicz and personally directed added scenes; Salesman Zanuck gave pep talks to branch managers; and Financier Zanuck exhorted exhibitors to advance millions in rentals for the blind booking of a picture that had not been completed and previewed.

Within a year the Skouras fils management of the Rivoli Theatre on Broadway where *Cleopatra* opened June 12, 1963 ("a monumental mouse"—Judith Crist, *New York Herald Tribune*) filed suit for damages to recover money for a picture fraudulently represented to be superior to any feature ever made by any studio anywhere: *Skouras vs. Skouras; Rivoli Theatre vs. Producer-Distributor; United Artists Theatres vs. Twentieth Century-Fox Film Corporation.*

Time, the great healer, has finally reversed the position of television, which for many years was a dirty word not mentioned publicly in some Hollywood studios: the devouring competitor which was giving away films for which theatres had to charge admissions to declining audiences.

The year 1966 was when television audiences proved conclusively that nothing that TV could originate had the appeal of a great movie that previously had played in theatres in fifty states. On Sunday night, September 25th, the American Broadcasting Company presented *The Bridge on the River Kwai* and blanketed both rival networks, a 50.8 Neilson rating indicating that the programming of Columbia Broadcasting System and National Broadcasting Company combined could not attract as many eyes and ears as that old Columbia Pictures release.

Three days later the same network, flushed with success, closed a deal with Twentieth Century-Fox to pay $19,500,000 for the right to videocast seventeen pictures (twice only). Included in this buy was *Cleopatra*—a windfall that, to scramble a metaphor, tipped the scales from red to black, since $5,000,000, added to theatre rentals, finally covered production and distribution costs.

Time, Zanuck and TV had, after six years, cured the

fiscal fiasco precipitated by the near-death of Elizabeth Taylor in London and her Roman holiday with another woman's husband. Walter Wanger, the producer whose contract called for 10 per cent of the net profit, had in 1962 sold a part of zero to Seven Arts Productions, which had liquid millions it was willing to gamble; and it now looks as if both the Wanger estate and Seven Arts, down through the years, will have a handsome annuity.

When *Cleopatra* had been launched in a series of hard-ticket engagements, Zanuck closed the huge Westwood, Malibu and Hollywood studios for eight months, cutting overhead by one third, settled contracts amounting to $3,620,671, wrote off stories and scripts for about $2,000,-000 and scrapped television distribution errors for $3,980,000.

Eight in-work pictures were completed, and President Zanuck, with his son Richard in charge of production, made a fresh start with seven new ones, including *The Sound of Music,* biggest financial success of all Fox pictures and *John Goldfarb,* the unfunny disaster.

"I'm the only head of a major studio," Zanuck told Mel Gussow in his world command post at the Hotel Plaza in New York, "except for Jack Warner, who ever had practical experience as a producer. I'm the president and I'm still the producer. That's the lifeblood of the industry. All the great salesmen don't mean anything. I have to make pictures or I'll be killed.

"I'm an unorthodox president. I delegate authority in every field. I hold the man responsible. I don't want to hear details. I don't want any whys and wherefores. I want to hear results."

Results he is now hearing, like the wonderful sound of money rolling in from all over the world from *The*

Sound of Music, "our miracle picture," with a world take for the distributor of more than $115,000,000, way ahead of *Gone With the Wind* and *The Ten Commandments.*

Results in his six golden years:

Net profits in 1968 of $13,752,000 or $1.95 per share.

Net profits in 1967 of $15,420,317 or $2.44 per share.

Net profits in 1966 of $12,504,000 or $4.28 per share.

Net profits in 1965 of $11,762,000 or $4.02 per share.

Net profits in 1964 of $10,565,000 or $3.61 per share.

Net profits in 1963 of $9,115,000 or $3.12 per share.

In this same interview in *New York* Magazine (then published Sundays by the *World Journal Tribune*) Zanuck contrasted his operations with those of Joseph E. Levine, president of Embassy Pictures: "Levine's a promoter, a package man. A good one! He puts things together and goes to lunch."

Zanuck rarely goes to lunch but has it brought to his hotel suite, where secretaries work in shifts until exhausted, taking voluminous dictation on what is wrong with every script; memos to his son in Century City; memos to producers in England, Ireland, Spain, Italy and Hong Kong.

The hotel switchboard can get London and Paris during their office hours after Zanuck's occasional nightclubbing, and there are hot lines to California and to Tenth Avenue in New York where vice presidents ride herd on global distribution.

Working in pajamas and mandarin robes, Zanuck makes his court-of-last-resort decisions, such as whether to write off the $4,000,000 preparation cost of *Bloomer Girl,* the votes-for-women period musical about Amelia Bloomer which ran for 654 performances on Broadway. Could Katharine Hepburn in bloomers (she has good legs) carry the load and make a profit? Or maybe the younger Shirley MacLaine, who can-canned for Khrushchev? Final decision: to scrap the production, charge the preparation cost to overhead, pay Shirley MacLaine $800,000 for not working plus legal costs in her suit for breach of contract signed August 6, 1965, for a grand total of about five million dollars.

Does the president of Procter & Gamble have to make such ulcerous decisions to meet Lever Brothers competition? Oh, for the relaxed days of independent production, when decisions on one or two pictures could be made at leisure.

"Sweat or go crazy. Get off or get on. Cancel or rewrite. The critical moment! Once you're embarked you're embarked. You can embellish with a cast, with photography, location work. But when you get to it the script is half of it. And before the script the subject matter. You can bluff, but your bluff will catch up with you. You can have all the campaigns you want, but when you get right down to it, it's do they want it? And if they don't want it, they don't care who says it's good."

As to his present and future, Zanuck admitted to Mel Gussow: "I don't say I like it now. I don't say I need it. The day will come, the day will certainly come, when I will step down as president and make a picture every year. I have no desire to be a permanent president."

27

INTO THE SUNSET

Westward the course of empire takes its way;
The first four acts already past,
A fifth shall close the drama with the day;
Time's noblest aspect is the last.

—GEORGE BERKELEY, 1730

As westward the course of empire, and of culture, takes its way, California, westernmost continental outpost, may well lay claim to being, for the final third of our century, time's noblest aspect.

Certainly no megalopolis has had more profound global influence on manners, morals, music, clothing, household furnishings and architecture than Los Angeles County, which has been exporting its culture, since the advent of cinematic sound, into the remotest tundra and jungle, where the natives, whether British royalty or Zulu tribesmen, are fascinated and influenced as ultimate consumers.

The cinema could hardly be what the Bishop of Cloyne (George Berkeley) had in mind, some 240 years ago, as time's noblest aspect, but technology has raced ahead, with its audio-visual impact, to make the moving picture "the only qualitative gain to communication since the alphabet was evolved," in the felicitous phrasing of B. A. Auginbaugh of the Ohio State Department of Education.

Television, after all, whether immediate with live performers, on tape or film, is only a quantitative gain in bringing Vision-by-Radio into the privacy of the home.

Westward, with culture primitively distributed from the library of Alexandria, westward to Athens, Rome, Paris, London. And, after the devastation of two world wars, the vast ocean leap to New York.

Westward the population center of the United States has moved from eastern Indiana, in the days of the nickelodeon to western Indiana, at Linton, with the advent of sound; to Olney, Illinois, in 1950, with national videocasting, and now, pausing on the banks of the Mississippi, at St. Louis, this nucleus vamps until population gains in Hawaii and Alaska pull it across Missouri to the U.S. geographic center and the North American geodetic center, both in Smith County, Kansas.

Westward in Los Angeles County, Fox is still working its way into the sunset, from the Sunset and Western studios built in 1910 by the founding father, to the Movietone City designed for sound by Earl Sponable and nursed along by Winfield Sheehan after the laying of the cornerstone in 1930.

But this acreage, sold to the Aluminum Company of America, has grown too valuable to sustain the overhead for theatre and television production. And so gradually, Fox moves into the sunset, over the Ringe Ranch sierras into Malibu acreage, now totaling 2,738, with the purchase in 1967 of the Ronald Reagan ranch from the farsighted governor of California, as part of the Westward Ho empire building of the astute Darryl Zanuck.

Despite the blundering and groping of the Fox management while Zanuck relaxed in Europe, time and technology were adding value to the company's real estate and negatives. In desperation the harassed President Skouras was forced to dip into the corporate grouch bag. Skouras, all his adult life an exhibitor, elected not to arouse the wrath of theatre owners by selling off television rights to his treasure trove of theatre features, their million-dollar negatives written off to one dollar by standard accounting practice. Reverberating in his ears was the exhibitor denunciation and threatened boycott of Paramount Pictures when Barney Balaban, a conservative penny-squeezer who ran Paramount like a bank, had in 1960 been forced, in order to make his balance sheet look good, to sell thirty Paramount pictures to Columbia Broadcasting System for six million dollars.

Since his various studio executives, under Skouras scrutiny, were unable to turn out profitable pictures, and since stockholders were demanding an end to recurring deficits, President Skouras decided to sell the Westwood real estate that President Fox had bequeathed him.

For many crucial months negotiations dragged on with the 91091 Corporation, one of the many far-flung enterprises of the now bankrupt William Zeckendorf, whose imagination outran his resources. (Fictional dialog as reported by irreverent newspaper commentators:
Son Z: We can close this deal for only sixty million.
Pop Z: Close it before they change their minds.
Son Z: But they want a sixty-thousand-dollar binder.
Pop Z: Forget it.)

Other promoters, including Marvin Kratter of New York, tried to swing a deal, until finally, April 17, 1961, the Aluminum Company of America paid Fox Realty Corporation $43,000,000 for its 99-year lease on 260 acres, and the studio leased back 75 acres at an annual rental of $1,500,000.

In his 1960 annual report President Skouras was able to
assure stockholders that the studio was now solvent. It
was his final favorable financial report before the curse of
Cleopatra dragged him down the up staircase to inactive
chairman of the board.

In 1967 Spyros Skouras announced, through the Securities and Exchange Commission, that he planned to sell
off some of his 112,510 shares, which leaves the Zanuck
holdings, with Darryl Zanuck voting 120,717 shares,
firmly in control. Indeed, just a week after he had been
heckled by stockholders about his son's salary at the
annual meeting May 17, 1967, Zanuck felt secure enough
to liquidate the executive vice president he had hired in
1963 and paid Seymour Poe about three million dollars
for his employment contract expiring August 22, 1968.

It was surmised that Poe might seem to outside stockholders the logical next president. But with Poe out of the
line of march, it will be more difficult for some corporate
raider (like those who tried to take over MGM) to scuttle
Richard Zanuck, if they were able to acquire the Skouras
stock and enough more in the open market to outvote
the Zanuck family block.

"If there is any corporate take-over, we'll do the taking,"
Darryl Zanuck has announced.

In July, 1967, when Jack Warner retired and his brother
Albert declined to serve on the board of the new Cana-
dian-dominated Warner Brothers–Seven Arts, Ltd., Darryl
Francis Zanuck became, with Scott Fitzgerald titling,
"The Last Tycoon."

Except for Adolph Zukor, the Hungarian immigrant
who at ninety-five is honorary chairman of the Paramount
he created and sold in 1966 to Charles G. Bluedorn, an
Austrian immigrant born when Zukor was in his second

half century, all the other founding fathers have made their exits: Marcus Loew, Carl Laemmle, William Fox, the brothers Cohn, and the brothers Warner, except for Jack.

From his command post, when his father retires, Richard Zanuck will be directing the world's greatest amusement complex, created by a Nineteenth Century Fox. This global empire is far bigger than Paramount, "the sleeping giant," now revitalized as a Gulf and Western subsidiary; bigger than the enormously prosperous studio-less United Artists, absorbed into Transamerica; more prosperous than Metro-Goldwyn-Mayer, with Fox 1966 earnings of $227 million as against MGM gross revenues of $184 million, although total Fox assets of $217 million were below Metro's $251 million.

Now thirty-five, Richard is executive vice president for world-wide production, and, according to producers and directors who have worked with both father and son, RDZ "is a better movie-maker than his father." They add that he is as creative as his father and gets along much better with people than DFZ, who was often a tyrant, swinging his polo club at his underlings.

This is no small tribute, since movie-making is much tougher today than in the father's twenty golden years.

"In Darryl's era," recalls talent chief Owen McLean, "we had a stable of seventy contract players and could cast a picture in an afternoon. Today's competition means that you are negotiating constantly, finding the right stories for them, putting intricate deals together to fit their tax problems and personal problems, filming the picture abroad if it suits them."

The complex logistics of filming and joint-venture production require intricate knowledge of deals and box-office values. With Twentieth Century-Fox supplying the financing, most producers have a 25 percent interest in total world profits. Such an arrangement can be very lucrative, as in the case of *The Sound of Music,* which has made producer Robert Wise independently wealthy.

This creative intelligence, compounded of luck, skill, technical know-how and an accurate reading of the public pulse, is what makes production so hazardous and so vastly profitable. As Darryl Zanuck has said:

"Ours is the only business in the world where your entire product walks out every night to sleep away from the studio. With this prime talent gone, what have we got? An obsolete head office building on Tenth Avenue in New York, twenty-two sound stages in Westwood, ten at Sunset and Western and three film laboratories. These are only tools. It takes talent, even genius, to operate these factories."

With stock market raiders active and envious traders swooping overhead, the Zanucks are not unaware that the personal empire now so profitable to them may one day be conglomerated into some holding company. As Richard has remarked: "Many big fish are after us. But if anything happens, it will most likely be with our blessing."

In a merger-minded world he is realistic about the present and what may happen in the seventies.

"I've seen the beating people in my position take from their superiors who know nothing about the picture business. If that should happen to me, I'll make pictures independently of such a conglomerate.

"My job now is really a young man's game, although

I am beginning to feel like an old man from the long hours and frustrations."

At the original Sunset and Western studio built by the founding father in 1910, Vice President William Self is turning out films for videocasting that have made Twentieth Century-Fox tops for four years in TV series film. Most of these outdoor action pictures, such as *Daniel Boone,* are ground out on the mountainous acreage of the Malibu ranch, where, one of these days, all production will be concentrated.

Westward the course of cinematic empire takes its way, thirty miles over the hills from the poorhouse, into the green pastures of Malibu, cradled between ocean sierras and the San Fernando Valley.

As the long shadow of William Fox projects into three centuries of the Fox companies, on which the sun never sets, take it from here, Richard, with the implied blessing of the Bishop of Cloyne, who used to ponder, back at Oxford, "on the prospect of planting Arts and Learning in America."

Many a scientist, in those air-conditioned think factories on the Leland Stanford campus, now outpoints quaint old Oxford in contemporary learning. Let Oxford dons rummage in their glorious past while you audio-visualize the future with the William Fox movietones.

With your own cinematic arts, and the Stanford pennant rampant, what obstacles can inhibit you from creating world culture, so that

> In happy climes, where from the genial sun
> And virgin soil such scenes ensue, ***
> There shall be sung another golden age,
> The rise of empire and of arts.

SIGNIFICANT FOX FILMS

1917 *Cleopatra,* starring Theda Bara, was a much better financial venture than the color-sound production forty-six years later, and within a year paid off with a handsome profit.

1920 *Over the Hill to the Poorhouse,* filmed at a cost of $100,000, returned a profit of $3,000,000, and was the most successful picture produced personally by the founding father.

1922 *A Fool There Was* launched the Theda Bara industry, as Theodosia Goodman was transformed into the vamping Theda Bara, whose "Kiss me, my fool" became a slogan adopted by lovers of that era. Starting at $150 a week, she starred in forty films, as her salary rose to $4,000 weekly. She retired in 1927, married director Charles Brabin, and from her Hollywood home watched the frantic transition to sound and television. She died in 1955.

1924 *The Iron Horse,* the outdoor epic dramatizing the union in 1869 of the Union Pacific, built by Irish gandy dancers, with the Central Pacific, forged by Chinese labor, was the first big picture directed by John Ford, who is the only director to have been honored by five Academy Awards.

1926 *What Price Glory* emerged as a smash silent picture from the Broadway stage success by Laurence Stallings and Maxwell Anderson to launch the starring careers of Victor McLaglen and Edmund Lowe. Directed by Raoul Walsh.

1927 *Sunrise,* in which F. W. Murnau introduced to Hollywood the traveling camera with such trail-blazing effects that it won the Academy Award for Outstanding Production, with the Cinematograph Award going to Charles Rosher and Karl Strauss.

1927 *Seventh Heaven* won the very first Photoplay Award, and Academy Awards went to Janet Gaynor as best actress, Frank Borzage as best director and the Writing Achievements Award to Benjamin Glazer for his script.

1929 *In Old Arizona,* the first all-talking feature produced outdoors, liberated the sound camera from the heavy insulation of studio stages, and pioneered location shooting.

1929 *The Cock-Eyed World* broke box-office records at the Roxy and elsewhere as Victor McLaglen and Edmund Lowe hurled their wartime obscenities at each other in a vocalization of Captain Flagg and Sergeant Quirt, who had pantomimed in *What Price Glory*.

1929 *Sunny Side Up.* With popular songs by De Silva, Brown and Henderson, Janet Gaynor and Charles Farrell sounded off with enormous international success, one instance being a Stockholm engagement of many months' duration that has never been topped in that theatre.

1930 *The Big Trail,* introducing the perennial John Wayne in the first wide-screen production at the Roxy Theatre, where this sound epic of covered wagon days was projected on 90 mm film in the Grandeur process owned 50/50 by William Fox and Harley Clarke, who succeeded Fox as president in a bankers' coup.

1933 *Cavalcade.* This distinguished production, directed by Frank Lloyd from the Noel Coward play about three generations of a British family, represented the artistic production peak for Winfield Sheehan, and won Academy and many other awards.

1940 *The Grapes of Wrath.* One of the all-time great pictures, directed by John Ford from Nunnally Johnson's script of the depression migration of the Okies, based on the novel by John Steinbeck.

1944 *Woodrow Wilson.* Not even the all-out production skills of Darryl Zanuck, propelled by big-budget advertising, could escalate this somewhat talky biography of the wartime president, directed by Henry King.

1953 *The Robe,* pioneering CinemaScope production using the squeeze and unsqueeze lenses of Henri Cretien, forced thousands of theatres to remodel with Miracle Mirror wide screens, and made a fortune for producer Frank Ross.

1957 *Peyton Place.* Jerry Wald's production of the Grace Metalious novel hit the $11,500,000 jackpot (United States and Canada) with Lana Turner starring, and spawned *Return to Peyton Place* ($4,500,000), in 1961.

1960 *Can-Can* came in for international attention when Premier Nikita Khrushchev and his hausfrau wife were outraged by Shirley MacLaine's gyrating thighs and pelvic closeups in glorious technicolor, causing President Skouras and Czar Eric Johnston, as hosts, to lose face.

1962 *The Longest Day.* Eddie Albert and Paul Anka help General Eisenhower win the second world war, with Darryl Zanuck riding herd on three directors, in one of the most complicated and Herculean pictures ever produced. Downgraded by Skouras, Zanuck had to fight the Greeks as well as the Germans for the ultimate victory of more than $35,000,000, of which DFZ collected his personal millions, in a percentage-of-the-profits deal.

1963 *Cleopatra,* with the curse of the Nile on both London and Rome, compounded by Elizabeth Taylor's sickness and passion for another woman's husband, sent Twentieth Century-Fox reeling toward bankruptcy, and ended the production career of Spyros Skouras. But thanks to TV and upcoming videocasting, its $43,000,000 production cost will eventually be recouped, although in 1969 it had not reached its break-even point with world rentals of $39,800,000.

1965 *The Sound of Music.* With an all-time Fox peak of $115,000,000 globally in 1969 (and more to come), this musical sings the sound of money.

1966 *Fantastic Voyage.* This fantastic special-effects accomplishment is a tribute to Producer Saul David and Director Richard Fleischer and especially to technicians L. B. Abbott, Art Cruickshank and Emil Rosa, Jr. How they managed to shrink Raquel Welsh and Stephen Boyd so that they could circulate alive through a human being's arteries and veins is one of those marvels of trick photography which the cinema alone can achieve.

1966 *The Bible.* Worth the price of admission just to see John Huston as Noah leading the animal kingdom into his ark, not to mention voyeurism with our ultimate grandmother, sans fig leaves, as she yields to the blandishments of the talking snake. Directed by Huston and produced in Italy by Dino De Laurentiis.

1967 *Dr. Dolittle.* Here again the special effects men worked their magic, with two-headed llamas and other odd fauna, but whether this magic can transcend the $17,000,000 production cost is still dependent on how many people stay away overseas. What price Rex Harrison?

1967 *The Valley of the Dolls* seems to be, on film and in the runaway novel, just what the public wants, with more than $26,500,000 rolling in, and author Jacqueline

Susann generously responding to public demand with (1969) *Beyond the Valley of the Dolls*.

1968 **Star.** The verdict is still out on this $12,000,000 production, despite the appeal of Julie Andrews ("the iron butterfly") and direction by Robert Wise. Gertrude Lawrence; who she? And, in retrospect, why?

INDEX